Ray Bradbury's
THE MARTIAN CHRONICLES

Walter James Miller
Professor of English, New York University

1998 Barnes & Noble Books

MACMILLAN is a registered trademark of Macmillan, Inc.
Monarch and colophons are trademarks of Simon & Schuster, Inc.,
registered in the U.S. Patent and Trademark Office.

Macmillan Publishing USA
A division of Simon & Schuster, Inc.
1633 Broadway
New York, NY 10019

ISBN 0-7607-1088-0

Text design by Tony Meisel

Printed and bound in the United States of America

98 99 00 01 02 03 M 9 8 7 6 5 4 3 2 1

RRDC

CONTENTS

RAY BRADBURY'S LIFE, TIMES, AND WORK

"FAMOUS OVERNIGHT"

Ray Bradbury's voice was low-key and easygoing as we talked about how *The Martian Chronicles* had made him famous, why he doesn't use a word-processor, how his novel in progress, *Falling Upward*, is based on memories of when, as a boy of fourteen, he skated to Hollywood every day.

> "I was autographing copies of *The Martian Chronicles* in a bookstore in Santa Monica," he was saying. "I recognized Christopher Isherwood when he walked in. Here was one of the leading authors of the day."

The English novelist Isherwood had moved to the United States in 1939 with the poet W. H. Auden, settled down near Hollywood, and become an American citizen in 1946.

> "I offered him a copy. I inscribed it to him. I thought I'd never hear from him again."

"But—?" I knew it was Isherwood who had "discovered" Bradbury, but I was hearing these personal details for the first time.

> "But! One night soon a friend called up. 'Isherwood wants to come over,' he said.

> " 'If he does, he'll have to sit on the floor,' I told him. 'Marguerite and I don't have any furniture yet in the living room.' "

By the time Isherwood arrived, bringing with him the Zen writer Gerald Heard, the Bradburys had pushed a chair into the parlor for the author of *Goodbye to Berlin*.

"Isherwood told me he had just become book-review editor of *Tomorrow* magazine," Bradbury recalled. "And he had decided that *The Martian Chronicles* would be the first book he reviewed.' "

The results are history. As James Gunn says in his authoritative critical anthology *The Road to Science Fiction*, "Isherwood 'discovered' Bradbury in the science fiction ghetto and announced his genius to the world." And Brian Aldiss, in his *Billion Year Spree: The True History of Science Fiction*, says "Isherwood announced that Bradbury was a poet. His name became famous overnight, and he has remained one of our eminent dreamers ever since, the Hans Christian Andersen of the jet age."

Bradbury added: "The next time Isherwood came over, he brought Aldous Huxley." A member of the great scientific family, Huxley was author of the 1934 SF (science fiction) classic *Brave New World*. Bradbury had arrived.

GENESIS OF THE CHRONICLES
"Norman Corwin was a name I hadn't heard in a long time," I probed. "Then I read in Wayne Johnson's *Ray Bradbury* that Corwin gave you the advice that led to your getting the *Chronicles* published."

I remembered a magnificent verse play Corwin had written, *On a Note of Triumph*. It was broadcast all over the world the day World War II ended. *Lord God of test-tube and blue print . . .* the lines came singing back to me.

"Corwin," Bradbury was saying, "had been a mentor throughout. In 1945, he was ready to introduce me to John Huston the film producer. I told Norman there was no way I could prove my love for Huston at that time.

"And in 1947, I tried out my ideas for 'Ylla' on Norman before I wrote it. I think I had read or told many of these stories to him. By 1949 I had all these science-fiction stories published in magazines but I still couldn't sell them as a book. Corwin urged me to go to New York and see several editors in person."

Johnson describes how Marguerite and Ray, expecting a child and low on funds, scraped together enough for him to make the four-day trip by bus. Enough for just a one-way ticket!

"I checked in at a YMCA dormitory for five dollars a week. William Bradbury (no relation), an editor at Doubleday, took me to eat at Luchow's." I remembered that landmark nineteenth-century restaurant, then located on 14th Street. "He wanted me to try working the Mars stories into a novel.

"I went back to the Y and worked until 2 a.m. I listed the Mars stories, arranged and rearranged them into a sequence that added up to a larger story, and realized all I had still to write were just little interchapters—such as John Steinbeck uses in *The Grapes of Wrath*."

"The critics usually say it was Sherwood Anderson's *Winesburg, Ohio* (1919) that gave you the idea of interchapters, or bridges between the stories," I commented.

"Oh yes, a friend had given me a copy of that back in 1944," And back in high school, I realized, Bradbury had taken a course in Hemingway, and so he was probably familiar too with Hemingway's linkage of his stories with little prose-poem-interchapters in *In Our Time* (1925).

"Next day I took my outline to Doubleday, and William gave me a $1500 advance for two novels." *The Martian Chronicles* would come out eight months later in 1950, *The Illustrated Man* in 1951.

Bradbury was halfway home on the bus before he realized he had enough money now to take the Pullman sleeper out to Los Angeles.

TAPPING THE UNCONSCIOUS

"How is it," I asked, "that more than most people, you can tap your memories all the way back to the day of your birth? Are you still using the free-association method you discovered forty-five years ago?" In his 1978 reissue of his 1957 novel *Dandelion Wine*, he tells how in his early twenties he had "floundered into a word-association process."

"You can do it," Bradbury told me, "if you start doing it and keep it up. You take a list of nouns, say:

> crickets
> attic
> night train

"You rummage through your mind. What do they mean to you?"

He had found that using this gimmick, especially immediately on waking up in the morning, produced memories of people that led him to dreaming up new situations that by day's end were new short stories. In his introduction to *The Stories of Ray Bradbury* (1980), he tells how just typing the words "The Playroom" led to fierce free-associations that in two hours became his SF horror story, "The Veldt."

"How's it working for you in *Falling Upwards*?" I asked.

> "I'm tapping my memories of the years I roller-skated to Hollywood, every day from my fourteenth to my seventeenth years. *Falling Upwards* is another *Tale of Two Cities*—the city of live stars in Hollywood, and the city of the dead stars in the graveyard nearby—Rudy Valentino, Douglas Fairbanks. . . ."

These memories were triggered for Bradbury when he used his word-association process on board ship en route to France in the mid-1980s.

"When I got to Paris I sat down at my battery-operated typewriter and banged out 150 pages in ten days." Almost four thousand words a day, I figured with envy.

A CHILD OF "POP" CULTURE

I realized, too, that I had just jotted down Bradbury's middle name. When Bradbury was born August 22, 1920, in Waukegan, Illinois, to Leonard Spaulding and Esther Moberg Bradbury, his mother, a habitual filmgoer, chose Douglas Fairbanks's first name as her son's middle name. An added example of how film was a strong and early influence, Ray Douglas Bradbury can recall seeing Lon Chaney in *The Hunchback of Notre Dame* when he was three years old. (But then that's nothing for a man who can recall seeing the scalpel the doctor used at his circumcision the day after he was born!)

Indeed, he credits his success as a creative artist to his having been brought up in the major forms of American "pop" culture—the horror movie, the carnival, the circus, the comics. When he was nine years old, he faced his first crisis as an artist. The Buck Rogers comic strip got off the ground that year. Ray Douglas fell in love with Buck's world and started collecting each day's installment. But some friends ridiculed his vulgar tastes. Embarrassed, he tore up his collection.

"For a month I walked through my fourth-grade classes, stunned and empty," he would recall in his introduction to *The Stories of Ray Bradbury*. "One day I burst into tears, wondering what devastation had happened to me. The answer was: Buck Rogers . . . was gone, and life wasn't worth living. The next thought was: those are not my friends, the ones who got me to tear the strips apart and so tear my own life down the middle: those are my enemies."

BEGINNING OF WRITING SF

He went back to collecting Buck Rogers strips. "My life has been happy ever since . . . that was the beginning of my writing science fiction. Since then, I have never listened to anyone who criticized my taste in space travel, sideshows, or gorillas."

BUT HIS WRATH, LIKE A VOLCANO. . . .

Nevertheless, happy or not, Bradbury cannot long contain his wrath at such "enemies." It erupts grandly every few years. His anger at censorship produced his classic SF horror story, "Usher II," one of the main events in the *Chronicles*. There you will see the part his pet "gorillas" play in his love of intellectual freedom. And in his introduction to his *Pillar of Fire and Other Plays*, he says that "Pillar of Fire" also

> . . . was caused by the quasi-intellectuals who mob through our society bullying us about our tastes, telling us that comic-strip cartoon books are bad for our digestion, worse for our imagination, and so should be burned. I would gladly Gunpowder Plot these ignorant social reformers out of existence, at least in my stories . . .

BRADBURY, HUXLEY, AND THE UNCONSCIOUS

If we compare Bradbury with Huxley, we can see how precocious Ray Bradbury was. At nine he had reached a point essential to adult individuation: he knew he had to trust his own tastes and break with those forces in our society that try to regiment our preferences. And at twenty he discovered ways to put his unconscious to work. But Aldous Huxley was over fifty when, in despair about the shallowness of his mental life, he began to experiment with drugs to bring his unconscious alive (as he tells us in *Doors of Perception*, 1954).

GOODBYE, WORD-PROCESSOR

I had noticed, in a biographical note about Bradbury that appeared in his novel *Death is a Lonely Business* (1985), that Bradbury took his first plane ride in his sixties. So I asked whether Bradbury, rather a rare SF writer with his antitechnological biases, uses a word processor in his writing.

"I don't want a machine doing my corrections. My errors are instructive to me," Bradbury answered. "I retype and the retyping gets me to revising. Also, I found out that it takes a week or two to learn how to use a word processor. So, when I got one as a gift, I finally gave it to my son-in-law."

BRADBURY ON THE MOON

I had one final question for Bradbury. This was about his celebrated minority opinion of the 1969 moon landing. Donald Wollheim, of Ace Books, asked twenty-seven SF writers to contribute their views on that historic event to his 1969 anthology *Men on the Moon* (1969). Surprisingly, only three SF authors—Philip K. Dick, Paul Anderson, and Bradbury—were full of praise for the space effort. The others took a skeptical view: e.g., they believed that the lunar walk brought "small cheer to the oppressed and impoverished on Earth," and that the Martians would become the "new Indians" (a fear further explored in this Monarch Note).

SOURCES OF BRADBURY'S OPTIMISM

Bradbury's celebrated (and, to some critics, controversial) optimism may be traced back to his apparently idyllic childhood. "I was a boy who did indeed love his parents and grandparents and brother," he tells us in the introduction to his 1975 edition of *Dandelion Wine*. This could be our cue to fill in those details of his career not already revealed in this account of our interview.

THE FORMATIVE YEARS

As we've seen, Bradbury's mother gave him intensive exposure to film and meanwhile, his teenage Aunt Neva read him Frank Baum's *Wizard of Oz* books when he was six. Stendhal and Pikes, characters in the *Chronicles'* "Usher," prove then to be two sides of Bradbury himself: the inveterate lover of fantasy in both the literary and cinematic media. His family also encouraged him to read Bullfinch's *Mythology*, and later he would recall that the Greek, Roman, and Norse myths ignited his passion for metaphor. From ages nine to twelve, he spent at least two nights a week in the Waukegan (Illinois) town library, "smelling the books like imported spices," as he tells us in his introduction to the 1967 edition of *Fahrenheit 451* (1953), "drunk on them before I read them." It was during those years he devoured the Tarzan and Mars novels of Edgar Rice Burroughs, without which *The Martian Chronicles* might never have been written.

A traumatic experience in Waukegan provided still another major subject for Bradbury's adult writing. One night, in his grandparents' house (next to his own), he discovered flame sweeping up one wall and eating at the ceiling. He was one of the bucket brigade that saved the house. Fire figures later as a malevolent force in the *Chronicles*, *Fahrenheit 451*, and other works. In his birthplace, Ray Douglas also developed his interest in acting, another major influence, which probably fostered his talent for writing dialogue.

THE TUCSON YEAR
The Bradburys moved to Tucson, Arizona, in 1932, and although they were there not much more than a year, he remembers it as one of the best years of his life. This twelve-year-old was on the radio one night a week "reading comic strips to the kiddies" (he was paid in tickets: the year of *King Kong* and *Dracula*), spending other nights singing in operettas, acting, and writing his first short stories.

"HEADED FOR LITERARY DISTINCTION"
The Bradburys moved again, in 1934, to Los Angeles. At Los Angeles High School he studied creative writing, perhaps came to appreciate poetic prose by reading Thomas Wolfe, and wrote some plays produced by the school dramatic society. The Los Angeles (LA) High 1938 yearbook summed up his past and his future with these lines under his photo:

> Likes to write stories
> Admired as a thespian
> Headed for literary distinction.

"EXTRA! EXTRA! READ ALL ABOUT IT!"

After graduating from LA High, Bradbury sold newspapers until he had saved enough money to buy a typewriter and rent an office in which to write. By his early twenties he was selling one horror story a month to *Weird Tales*, detective stories to *Dime Mystery*, and science fiction to *Planet Stories* and *Super Science Stories*. In 1944, he published forty stories but earned only $800. Then, in his mid twenties, when he was living in the Chicago section of LA (part of the setting in *Death is a Lonely Business*, 1985), his style matured into his now characteristic poetic prose, and he sold to the "slicks"—*Collier's, Mademoiselle, Charm, American Mercury*. 1947 was a major turning point in his life: he and Marguerite Susan McClure were married, and Arkham House (publishers of H. P. Lovecraft) issued his first book, *Dark Carnival*, a collection of twenty-seven of his tales from the pulp magazines. This fills in the background up to the points covered in the interview with Ray Bradbury. His major literary works are listed in the Selected Bibliography.

MAN OF MANY GENRES

Since he sold his first story to *Weird Tales*, at the age of twenty, Bradbury has published more than five hundred stories, novels, plays, screen plays, and poems, maybe half of which have found their way into his eighteen books. His screen plays include episodes for television shows like *The Alfred Hitchcock Hour* and *The Twilight Zone*, two SF movies: *It Came from Outer Space* and *The Beast from 20,000 Fathoms*, and the script for John Huston's *Moby Dick*. (Yes, he finally did feel he could prove his love for Huston.) Of his stage plays, *The World of Ray Bradbury* and *The Wonderful Ice Cream Suit* did well in Los Angeles and the latter had a short run off-Broadway.

FILM VERSIONS OF THE FICTION

In 1967, Francois Truffaut produced an adaptation of Bradbury's *Fahrenheit 451*. Two years later Jack Smight made a film out of three stories from *The Illustrated Man*. In 1972, *Picasso Summer*, a film version of Bradbury's "In a Season of

Calm Weather," appeared on television. And in 1980, perhaps the worst cinematic version of Bradbury yet, a television play by Richard Matheson called *The Martian Chronicles*, which ran as a two-part miniseries.

The Beast from 20,000 Fathoms, Fahrenheit 451, The Illustrated Man, and *The Martian Chronicles* (like *Moby Dick*) are all occasionally revived on television. Only *Fahrenheit 451* has won enthusiastic praise from Bradbury himself (he didn't even like Gregory Peck's interpretation of Ahab in *Moby Dick*).

BRADBURY AND TECHNOLOGY

Meanwhile, our author has had a more favorable impact on noncinematic technology and exploration. His services as idea consultant were eagerly sought for the United States Pavilion at the 1964 World's Fair, and since then he has also done consulting work in city engineering and rapid transit. And when one of the Apollo teams landed on the moon, they named Dandelion Crater after Bradbury's novel *Dandelion Wine*.

WHAT'S AHEAD

This interview and survey of related materials have given us the biographical information about Bradbury we need for a full appreciation of *The Martian Chronicles*. Next we'll look into the part Mars has played in popular science, in SF before Bradbury, and as a setting for his novel. We'll survey the meaning of the *Chronicles* and the techniques Bradbury has used to drive his meaning home. We shall conclude with a chapter-by-chapter analysis of the *Chronicles* (a detailed study of the plot, the themes, the style), some topics for papers, and reports, and a selective biography of works by and about Ray Douglas Bradbury.

MARS: IN SCIENCE, IN EARLIER SF, AND IN BRADBURY

FOCUS ON MARS

In their fascinating book *Life Beyond Earth*, theoretical physicist Gerald Feinberg and biochemist Robert Shapiro note that:

> The planet Mars has been the main focus of scientific studies and of speculative literature about extraterrestrial life, at least for the last century.

Inevitably, they include Bradbury as one of the three leading authors of that literature. They say "at least for the last century" presumably because, before that, the main focus was on the moon. They go on

> . . . many scientists believe that some of the other bodies in the solar system may prove to be better homes for life . . .

Why then has Mars become the main focus? What relationship is there between the Mars that scientists study and the Mars that writers speculate about? To what extent has Bradbury attempted to be scientific in *The Martian Chronicles?*

What has he contributed to our thinking about the nature and effects of interplanetary exploration? SF writers have often made stunning prophecies that came true. Can we credit Bradbury with any successful predictions about Mars—or Earth? And not so incidentally—why do Feinberg and Shapiro call writings about Mars by H. G. Wells, Edgar Rice Burroughs, and Ray Bradbury speculative literature? Writings we normally call science fiction, sci-fi, science fantasy, SCI/FAN, or—SF?

CANALS ON MARS?

From ancient times, Earth dwellers have always considered Mars outstanding among the heavenly bodies because of its blood-red color. For the same reason, the Romans named it after their god of war. For generations modern astronomers have tried to map Mars. The German Wilhelm Beer (1797–1850) produced the first map of "the Red Planet" that resolved its surface into light and dark areas. The Englishman Richard Proctor (1837–1888) refined these areas into continents, seas, bays—and named them. Then, in 1877, when Mars and Earth came within thirty-five million miles of each other, two events occurred that made the neighbor planet a topic of everyday conversation. A professor at the United States Naval Observatory in Washington, Asaph Hall (1829–1907), discovered two tiny moons revolving around Mars. And the director of the Bresa Observatory in Italy, Giovanni Schiaparelli (1835–1910), mapped networks of crisscrossing straight lines he perceived on the Martian surface. He called them *canali*, an Italian word meaning channels or canals but intended in this case to denote natural surface features. His word was mistranslated into English to denote clearly artificial structures. The popular press exploited this mistake to report that canals discovered on Mars proved there was life there, life of such high intelligence it could design and operate the largest system of artificial waterworks ever known anywhere.

LOWELL'S MARS

The sensational press reports excited an astronomer wealthy enough to pursue the question. Percival Lowell (1855–1916) set up his own private observatory in Arizona. From thousands of photographs he took of Mars' surface, he drew detailed maps of some five hundred canals extending for thousands of miles. He called the places where his straight lines intersected, and in some places he saw double parallel lines—oases.

In 1906 Lowell—a member of the family that has produced the poets Amy and Robert Lowell—published *Mars and Its Canals*, and in 1909 *Mars as the Abode of Life*. As Isaac Asimov puts it, this sanctified Lowell as "the patron saint of the intelligent-life-on-Mars cult."

The canals were necessary, Lowell explained, because the Martian seas and rivers had dried up and the planet's engineers had to channel water from the polar ice caps out to the rest of Mars. Because it is tilted (like Earth), and has a long elliptical orbit (longer than Earth's), Mars has seasons. And so when the north polar ice cap melts, Lowell pointed out, the water is channeled south; when the southern ice mass thaws, the water in the canals reverses direction. The Martian technologists had taken on an engineering project so enormous that "the supposed vast enterprises of the Earth," he said, "look small beside it." And people so expert in construction obviously had also built great cities. The planet clearly had been misnamed: it could not be the abode of a warlike race. Only a people united in peace could have worked in such global harmony.

"LAST-DITCH EFFORTS"

Even so, their canals were merely delaying actions, literally last-ditch efforts, because Mars was not only drying out but dying out. Lowell's descriptions of the noble, doomed Martians, living on deserts swept by sandstorms, now engaged the imagination of writers of adventure stories published in the pulp magazines, and even of novelists considered more artistic.

GETTING TO MARS

Meanwhile, other scientists were working on the means of getting to other heavenly bodies. The Russian Konstantin Tsiolkovsky (1857–1935) laid down the mathematical theory for rocket propulsion; the German Hermann Oberth pioneered in rocketry experiments; the American Robert Hutchings Goddard (1882–1945) built the prototypes for the Space Age vehicles.

SCIENCE BY 1948

We need to add just one more scientific discovery to complete our outline of what was known about Mars and space travel at the time Bradbury was working on *The Martian Chronicles*. In 1948 the Dutch-American astronomer Gerard Kuiper (1905–1973) discovered that the atmosphere of Mars is predominantly carbon dioxide.

SCIENCE FICTION BY 1948

Meanwhile, how had SF figured on questions of Mars and outer space at the time Bradbury was chronicling Mars? Before going into the details, it is important to make one generalization about a situation already well known by 1948: A crossfertilizing process between science fiction and science facts was already underway. Many Space scientists-Tsiolkovsky, Oberth, the German-American Wernher von Braun (1912–1977), and others said they had been inspired by the SF of Jules Verne (1828–1905); Goddard attributed his inspiration to the SF of H. G. Wells (1866–1945). In other words, some of the prophecies made by SF are self-fulfilling.

That these leading thinkers, and top scientists in other fields as well, drew inspiration from SF would indicate to any objective observer that SF must reach high levels of intellectual and theoretical discourse. The opposite was true. In 1948, there was still considerable disdain for SF in the academic and literary Establishments. This was one of the reasons Isherwood's judgment of Bradbury (see Chapter 1) was so important in the history of literature.

DEFINING SF

In his four-volume *The Road to Science Fiction*, our major SF anthology, James Gunn jokes about the innumerable definitions so far attempted: by now, he says, one person's definition of SF is just as good as anybody else's. But maybe we could get everyone to agree on this minimal definition:

> SF is fiction that assumes some imaginary scientific advance and/or some great change in the human environment, and explores the possible consequences.

But even this basic description invites fierce controversy. Some SF writers and critics insist a story is not true SF unless it emphasizes highly technical processes.

The vexed question of what writings are to be labeled "hard" or "soft core," or "science fantasy" ultimately clouds our enjoyment of their literary qualities and of the meaning and significance of their themes. For our purposes here let's say: *The Martian Chronicles* certainly assumes imaginary scientific advances and great changes in the human environment, and it certainly explores some of the consequences. But the consequences Bradbury chooses to emphasize are more often in the realm of the social sciences than that of the physical sciences. Bradbury's work is good SF for different reasons from Verne's—or Jerry Pournelle's. If you are interested in working out more detailed classifications of SF writers, you will enjoy Gunn's introduction to volume one of *The Road to Science Fiction* and Brian Aldiss's *Billion Year Spree*. Bradbury figures in Aldiss's classification, and is praised by Gunn.

SHOULD SF MEAN SPECULATIVE FICTION?
Now we have a better idea of why two leading scientists, Feinberg and Shapiro, prefer to talk about speculative fiction. It includes any fiction—Verne, Pournelle, Bradbury, Huxley—that speculates on the possibility of scientific and environmental change and its consequences.

SF ABOUT MARS BY 1948
What had SF done about subjects important to Bradbury when he was working on his book about Mars and space exploration? Verne had established many of the features of space travel—escape velocity, the shape of the capsule, and splashdown, for instance—and had also established the inescapable connection between science and social science (*From the Earth to the Moon* and *All Around the Moon, 1865–1970*). Wells started work on his *The War of the Worlds* (1898) on the basis of Schiaparelli's networks of lines, a hot topic during the international studies of 1894, when Mars again came within thirty-five million miles of Earth. Wells mentions Schiaparelli's "markings . . . mapped so well" in his opening pages. But his Martian monsters are far beyond canals—they're into spaceships. They invade England, and Wells's stupefied Englishmen are saved only by interplanetary contagion: his Martian troops succumb to Earth bacteria with which their systems have had no experience.

A clue to how Americans might react to invasion from outer space came in 1938 when a radio dramatization of *Worlds* by Orson Welles—presented as a newscast—had New Yorkers and other sophisticates in panic on the streets, and then out on the highways north—for the Martians had "landed" in New Jersey.

BURROUGHS'S MARS

If Wells followed up on Schiaparelli, then Edgar Rice Burroughs followed hard upon Lowell. Just three years after the astronomer had published his *Mars as the Abode of Life*, Burroughs serialized his novel *Under the Moons of Mars* in *All-Story* magazine (1912; it appears in paperback still as *A Princess of Mars*). Of his seventy books, eleven are set on Mars, including *The Gods of Mars* (1918), *The Warlords of Mars* (1919), *The Chessmen of Mars* (1922), and *The Synthetic Men of Mars* (1940). Burroughs's Martians live on a planet such as Lowell described (they call it Barsoom): its seas have dried up, canals are used to circulate water. But the Martians themselves are not as Lowell imagined. Burroughs disregarded Lowell's inferences that Mars is pacifistic. Burroughs's Martians never go unarmed and are at war constantly. The Princess is red-skinned; some fifteen footers are green, four-armed, tusked; there are white Martians too. Most of Burroughs's Martians have little need for fine language because they can communicate telepathically. (Most of Burroughs's literary critics complain that he himself had little need of fine language to make ten million dollars on Mars and Tarzan.)

Among other writers turning out SF stemming from Lowell's concepts were Leigh Brackett (1915–1978) and her husband Edmond Hamilton (1904–1977).

And among all of these who have influenced Bradbury's *Chronicles* we should mention Aldous Huxley (1894–1963), grandson of scientist Thomas Henry Huxley (1825–1895), whose futuristic novel *Brave New World* is a utopian nightmare (or, as we shall see later, a dystopian novel) in which scientific progress is treated as a vain deceit. Life has become standardized and mechanized; only those people on Earth untouched by progress still enjoy integrity and hope.

ENTER RAY BRADBURY

How did Bradbury pick and choose from the scientists and science-fiction writers available to him as influences? Bradbury's Martian environment is Lowellian: its seabeds and riverbeds are dry, deserts and dust storms persist through changes in seasons; his Martians are Lowellian too: builders of great canals, great cities, a pacifistic people whose planet and civilization are in decline. Bradbury has also assumed all of the advances implicit in the rocketry pioneering by Tsiolkovsy, Oberth, Goddard, von Braun; and his descriptions of the Martian atmosphere are in accordance with the latest (1948) studies by Kuiper.

HIS SF INFLUENCES

Aside from accepting Verne's notions about escaping gravity and voyaging through space, Bradbury's main debt to the Father of Science Fiction seems to be Verne's assumption that scientific advances can be explored only in a context of social change. From Wells, Bradbury got the precedent for planetary contagion: whereas Well's Martians are destroyed by bacteria they encounter on Earth, Bradbury's are nearly wiped out by viruses brought to Mars by Earth people. As we shall see in our textual analysis, there are other twists in the interplanetary contagion implicit in one of Bradbury's late chapters. And from Wells, Bradbury certainly got much encouragement for thinking about the Martians as people who could develop vehicles that do not move on wheels but on means of locomotion more organic than mechanical.

Burroughs, however, was Bradbury's main inspiration, because Burroughs had excited Bradbury from childhood on, when he devoured the Barsoom books and the Tarzan comics. "Without Edgar Rice Burroughs, *The Martian Chronicles* would never have been born," Bradbury says. In Burroughs's work, Bradbury could see ways to use the Lowellian landscape: the natural dryness and the artificial waterways. From Burroughs,

Bradbury also borrows telepathy as one of the Martians' means of communication but, as we shall see, with many subtle modifications of his own creation, Bradbury instinctively rejected two aspects of Burroughs' SF. Bradbury's Martians are not monstrous and warlike but beautiful and peace-loving. Bradbury also rejects the temptation to write so hastily, so shallowly, as did the creator of Barsoom. Bradbury affectionately refers to Burroughs as a "vulgarian" but the Chronicler of Mars allows none of that aspect in his own work.

Rather like his friend Leigh Brackett, Bradbury took much of his matter from Burroughs but learned his manner from greater literary artists—Wells, Sherwood Anderson, Norman Corwin, Edgar Allan Poe.

Finally, as we analyze Bradbury's text chapter by chapter, we shall see that he has been strongly influenced in his thinking by the Aldous Huxley school of dystopian writers.

RB'S ORIGINALITY AND PROPHECIES

In addition to originally developing the Verne-Wells concepts of the social functions of SF, Wells's ideas on locomotion and contagion, and SF's stock ideas on telepathy, Bradbury can be credited with many more new SF ideas, many of which have proved prophetic. In the *Chronicles* he explores the nature of the human sensation of time, and our need to extend our life span so as to capitalize on the wisdom of advanced age. He quietly assesses dramatic possibilities such as channeling lava for its enormous heating potential, and solar energy to run a house just as a flower opens, turns, and closes with the sun's movements.

He correctly foresaw, in 1950, the development of such comforts as the cassette player, the water bed, the answering machine, the transparent pack(age), and such possibilities as determining the sex of the human fetus. In the same year, he also correctly predicted social developments: the rise of McCarthyism, movements like the Moral Majority, the military control of the space effort; the United States policy (forty years after he wrote the *Chronicles*) of "downplaying international cooperation" in exploring Mars, "stressing that the main objective is to assert American leadership in space" (*New York Times*, March 29, 1987).

ENTER THE CRITICS

We'll invoke the aid of several critics in our textual analysis of the *Chronicles* (Chapter 5). Here, though, it is essential to wind up our discussion of the science in Bradbury's work by answering a few unfair charges by the critics, and by updating a few facets of the ever-developing scientific view of Mars.

James Gunn says in volume 3 of his critical anthology, *The Road to Science Fiction*, that "Bradbury's Mars clearly was impossible even when he began to write it in 1946." Gunn's eagerness to deride Bradbury made him overlook some data in the history of science. Of course, today we know that canals do not exist on Mars. But according to Feinberg and Shapiro, as late as the early 1960s . . . canals were not fully eliminated from consideration. And *The Martian Chronicles* appeared in 1950, well within the period when canals were certainly not considered "impossible." True, in the 1960s and 1970s improved telescopes showed that Lowell's long straight lines are really quite broken and irregular, while the Mariner spacecraft took closeup photos showing no Martian features at all resembling Lowell's canals. But we now know that the older terrain of Mars's southern hemisphere does have numerous channels tens of miles wide and hundreds of miles long. These channels strongly suggest that there once was a liquid element, possibly water, on Mars' surface. Although two Viking probes of Mars in 1976 found no life (in the tiny areas in which they operated), they did discover that "Mars, of all the nearby planets, has conditions most hospitable to human habitation" (*New York Times*, March 29, 1987).

How did Schiaparelli and Lowell ever make such a mistake as seeing long, straight, intersecting lines all over Mars? The science of optics can explain the error. It seems that when we strain to resolve objects at the far reaches of our vision, irregular blotches there affect our eyes as interconnecting straight lines. And so Proctor's "continents" became Lowell's "crisscrossings"!

Answering William F. Touponce's gaffe in his *Ray Bradbury and the Poetics of Reverie* will also allow us to continue to downgrade Gunn's "impossible." Touponce says the *Chronicles* "bears no resemblance to the known scientific facts about Mars except that it is the next planet out from our sun after Earth." True, Bradbury establishes that in his very first chapter. But he also makes clear, repeatedly throughout, that: Mars's atmosphere has less oxygen and more carbon dioxide than Earth's air has; that Mars has two moons, seasons, deserts, and dust storms, for a total of six resemblances to the known scientific facts about the third planet.

THE BOTTOM LINE

Actually Bradbury's novel doesn't stand or fall on the viability of some of its science. What he's done is use Mars as a convenient outpost for examining what the American character reveals about itself when it's posted way, way out. As we've shown earlier, the *Chronicles* meets the basic definition of SF. (True, it is better to call it *speculative fiction*.) But the *Chronicles* is also a work of mythopoeia, i.e., Bradbury is remaking old myths and trying to shape new ones. Apparently the public understands that as well as many of the critics (e.g., see Robert Scholes and Eric Rabkin, Brian Aldiss, Jack Sullivan in the "Selected Bibliography") because at this writing they have bought more than six million copies of *The Martian Chronicles*.

BRADBURY'S THEMES IN
THE MARTIAN CHRONICLES

THEMES: EXPLICIT AND IMPLICIT

During and after an experience with good fiction, we naturally reflect on its subject, central ideas, thesis, message, moral, its overall meaning. And pulling together all the conclusions we can derive from a story, we find it convenient to designate them with a catchall word: themes. We sometimes refer to one aspect of a theme, a subtheme, as a motif. We may consider our inferences to be valid if our formulations of the themes and motifs prove to be interrelated and overlapping.

Sometimes an author states his themes explicitly, outright, either in his own authorial voice (e.g., Upton Sinclair in *The Jungle*) or, more subtly, through his characters' own statements of their beliefs and conclusions. Thus, many of Bradbury's themes can be found in dialogue involving Stendhal ("Usher II"), William ("The Million-Year Picnic"), Spender and Wilder ("—And the Moon Be Still as Bright"). We know that Bradbury intends their intellectual observations to be thematic because he makes them all sympathetic characters. We know the author does not intend us to take our philosophy of life from the speeches of Parkhill ("The Off Season") or Garrett ("Usher II") because he makes them unattractive: their ideas seem to be inherent in their unpleasant personalities.

At other times the author will use the most subtle, most artistic means of thematizing: He allows us to derive his meaning from the conduct and fate of his characters, from the outcome of their action. Thus, we learn about Bradbury's view of a certain type of businessman from Parkhill's behavior, and the author's attitude toward repressive bureaucracy from the fate of Stendhal and Pikes ("Usher II") and of Wilder ("The Off Season," "The Long Years"). Let us say that such themes are expressed implicitly. Bradbury seems to offer these ideas, explicit or implicit, as his main themes in the *Chronicles*.

METAMORPHOSIS

All literature involves change; without change we have no story, no drama. Bradbury's concern with metamorphosis is in finding its cause and using these findings as a lesson, maybe even a warning. Being flexible enough to confront change, to face the new with equanimity, with an open mind, can lead Bradbury characters to growth and survival ("The Martian," "—And the Moon Be Still as Bright," "The Million-Year Picnic"). Being unable to interact with change leads them to tragic mistakes ("Ylla," "The Off Season," "The Earth Men"). Metamorphosis is inevitable but in Bradbury's fiction, it is emphatically more favorable when it is under control or at least under scrutiny. The Martians were able to halt technological advance at the right point in their history; the Americans were not. Bradbury's Martian civilization lasts for tens of thousands of years, while his Americans blow themselves up in a few centuries.

EFFECT OF MACHINERY ON PERSONALITY

Before Bradbury's Americans atomize their home planet, they have already developed machinery to the point where they spend almost all their time coordinating their every movement with the action of their appliances! Their life, as we infer from "There Will Come Soft Rains," has become so routinized and prescheduled that they must have lost all imagination and spontaneity. And their machinery destroys the Nature that nurtures them. By contrast, the Martians have developed machines that are so beautiful, so unintrusive, so in harmony with Nature, that they foster the imagination and enjoyment of life.

EFFECTS OF REPRESSION

In several chapters, Bradbury explores the effects of repression of the imagination, and of individual freedom, by male chauvinism ("Ylla"), by governmental agencies ("Usher II"), and by racists ("Way in the Middle of the Sky"). In every case, repression leads either to a breakdown of a personality or to revolution, bloodless or bloody. By contrast, the Martians are so individually advanced in sociopolitical matters that they have no need for leaders ("The Off Season").

EFFECTS OF THE WORK ETHIC

Bradbury represents the work ethic, enforced by male-dominated society on both Earth and on Mars, as destructive to imagination and love. Until William settles on Mars, he has never had much time to spend with his boys ("The Million-Year Picnic"). Ylla recommends that his wife cure her imagination by immersing herself in work ("Ylla").

AMERICAN VALUES

Americans and their value systems are under continuous attack in the *Chronicles*. One of the functions of SF is to provide us with new ideas from alternative worlds. The most compact and explicit summary of America's faults is given in the Spender-Cherokee and Spender-Wilder dialogues ("—And the Moon Be Still as Bright"), in William's speeches ("The Million-Year Picnic"), and in "The Taxpayer" monologue, all directly inspired by American policies. But the following criticisms are at least implicit throughout the book:

> Americans have little respect for any values different from their own; they have little curiosity about, or ability to learn from, other cultures. If possible, they prefer to colonize and exploit other peoples rather than live in cooperation and harmony with them. Americans cherish business and militaristic values at the expense of health and the environment, art, the humanities, peace, and other humanitarian concerns. They develop technology without any concomitant development of ethics, esthetics, political science, psychology, diplomacy. They create false dichotomies between life and art, science and religion, mental and physical life, technology and Nature. They foster a tyranny of the mediocre majority over any talented minority. In Spender's phrase, Americans are "greedy, righteous bigots" ("—And the Moon Be Still as Bright").

EFFECT OF POINT OF VIEW ON PERCEPTION

Americans and Martians both suffer from the way their points of view distort their perception of reality. Of course, SF is the ideal medium for exploring this universal problem, since its characters are forced to cope with totally unfamiliar situations. In the opening story in *Chronicles*, a Martian, who lives in a carbon-dioxide atmosphere, says categorically there cannot be life on Earth because it has too much oxygen in its air! His wife cannot separate her sexual fantasy from some objective, vital, epoch-making information about Earthlings nearby. In "The Earth Men," the Martians classify the new arrivals with hundreds of insane people who also claim to have come from other planets. And the Earth men contribute to their own predicament by persisting in expecting a hero's welcome when it is long obvious there is a tragic problem here in extraterrestrial, extramartian communication: We are locked into our own narrow background and experience and, under pressure from the work ethic and other repressive forces, we cannot maintain an open mind or postpone judgment.

SUMMARY OF THEMES

Bradbury's themes add up to this message: Earthlings, Americans especially, cannot survive unless they respect and learn from other cultures; abandon their tradition of subjugation and exploitation of beings different from themselves; abandon the work ethic in favor of enjoyment of life for its own sake; redirect their technology toward humane goals; and harmonize with rather than destroy Nature. Bradbury makes it clear that arriving at these new values is not so much a function of intellect as it is a matter of basic decency. True, the intellectual Captains Black and Wilder are open minded and humanitarian, but so are Pop and Gomez, those lovable members of the working class in "The Martian."

We shall explore all these themes at greater length in Chapter 5, "Chapter-by-Chapter Textual Analysis."

PLOT STRUCTURE, TECHNIQUES, AND STYLE

OTHER FACTORS IN BRADBURY'S SUCCESS

As we have demonstrated, Bradbury's boldness in addressing some of the major themes of our era is surely one factor in his fame as a writer. Other factors equally important are his superb control of form—that is, the way he excites our curiosity and then deeply satisfies it; creation of memorable characters, both three-dimensional ("round") and two-dimensional ("flat"), whose dialogue is a joy to hear; combination of the techniques of SF, black humor, the horror story, and "slick" and mainstream fiction, a combination that raises many of his stories to the level of "art" fiction; lyrical language which, despite its richness, still advances the action steadily and, because of its richness, raises many passages to the level of the prose poem.

PLOT: MYTHIC STRUCTURE, PLUS

As we have seen in chapter I, Bradbury created the novel *The Martian Chronicles* by selecting about half of his short stories about Mars, converting and arranging them into fourteen chapters, dated in chronological order, then cementing them together with a dozen interchapters. The resulting twenty-six chronicles follow a traditional mythic pattern, but one with an ironic twist and one significant addition.

A typical myth falls into three parts: 1) the heroes' departure in search of adventures; 2) the adventures; then 3) either the return home of heroes now better able, as a result of their adventures, to take up their duties in the home community, or their settling down in a new home discovered during their journeys and adventure. If we survey Bradbury's action in these terms, we also discover a three-part structure:

> 1. In his first six chronicles, from "Rocket Summer" to "The Third Expedition," Bradbury recounts the efforts

and failures of the first three expeditions to "the Red Planet."

2. In his next thirteen chronicles, from "—And the Moon Be Still as Bright" through "The Martian," he narrates the successes of later expeditions and the waves of migration.

3. Now the original intention of these migrants is not returning home, but settling down. However, because of wars on Earth, they are, ironically, obliged to give up Mars and make the unintended journey back home. Bradbury recounts this—and the aftermath on both planets—in the next six chronicles from "The Luggage Store" to "There Will Come Soft Rains."

The three-part mythic story has come to a tragic close. But now Bradbury adds an epilogue, or, as we would call it in a musical composition, a *coda* (tail-piece), an optional extension of, or a supplement to, the original subject matter. With Mars abandoned and life wiped out on Earth, just one family manages to escape Earth to attempt, on a much smaller scale, the same mythic (1, 2, 3) cycle all over again ("The Million-Year Picnic").

INTERCHAPTERS
Some critics call the interchapters "bridges." Later we shall call some of them "preludes" or "interludes," according to their varying functions. But Bradbury's own word for them, as we learned in our interview with him, is interchapters, a concept he says he borrowed from Steinbeck and Anderson, and very likely from Hemingway too (see Chapter 1).

DISTINCTION BETWEEN CHAPTERS
AND INTERCHAPTERS
Our textual analysis (Chapter 5) will reveal interesting artistic distinctions between the interchapters and the chapters.

Each interchapter gives us a broad overview of the changing situation in Earth-Mars relations. It generalizes about the people involved. Usually it does not focus on any specific individuals, they are simply symbolic "walk-ons," serving a brief need in the overall picture, not at all developed as characters.

By contrast, each chapter gives us closeup views, focuses on specific people in specific, local situations, and develops the main character(s) involved.

The alternation of interchapter—vignettes with chapter—stories provides a great variety of reading experiences, a kind of cinematic experience, with views ranging from closeups to "establishing shots," action seen from many different camera angles, paced with lots of "crosscutting."

INDIVIDUAL STORY STRUCTURE

Bradbury is a master of the short-story form. Indeed, he helped perfect it during the heyday of the great American "general" magazines that used to feature fiction in every issue. He begins a story in classical *in medias res* fashion (i.e., *in the midst of things*), so close to the climax that we expect it momentarily. All background situations and previous action (exposition) he communicates to us through flashbacks which may be staged in a character's mind or in dialogue. He complicates the rising action steadily until it achieves its main crisis, the point of final commitment from which there's no turning back, and he prolongs this high-tension conflict until it reaches its climax and falling action, or resolution.

For appreciation of Bradbury's techniques of exposition, study the way he gives us the background situation in "The Long Years," as Hathaway moves from his "family" indoors to the Martian graveyard, to discovery of the red light in the sky; and "Usher II," in which all background information is laid out for us in Stendhal's dialogues and interior monologues.

For appreciation of Bradbury's handling of the conflict to crisis to climax sequence, study "The Martian," from the moment he is found by LaFarge in his new form as Lavinia, as he struggles in conflict with LaFarge and with himself, agonizes through a long crisis—with Spaulding, the police, the crowd—to the climax, which is followed by a very brief falling action. Note that in Bradbury, as always in the twentieth-century plot story, the action not only begins close to the climax (twenty-four hours away in "The Martian"), but also the climax is close to the end.

CONFLICT

What generates the action, of course, is conflict. The artistic writer multiplies the tensions in his story or play by developing conflict on several levels. Thus in "—And the Moon Be Still as Bright," Bradbury depicts a physical or social conflict between groups (different groupings of the crew at different times), an ideological conflict (Spender versus the crew, Spender versus Wilder, Wilder versus Parkhill), and a psychological conflict in Spender's mind (as he wavers between determination to kill for Mars and revulsion from his killings).

In some stories, Bradbury manages to maintain strong interest without internal (psychological) conflict. Thus, "Usher II" and "Way in the Middle of the Air" are propelled by social conflict (between Stendhal-Pikes and the censors; between the escaping blacks and the racist whites) and by ideological conflict (between authoritarianism and personal liberty; between racist theory and egalitarian theory). Only near the end of "Way in the Middle of the Sky" can we detect—and then only from the outside—any psychological conflict (as some of the men struggle between their fear of Teece and their newly generated tolerance of the blacks). For more authentic examples of fully developed internal conflict, reread "Ylla" (for hers) and "The Million-Year Picnic."

LINKAGE

Usually an author achieves continuity and unity by keeping at least one character on stage all the way through (e.g., Jordan in Hemingway's *For Whom the Bell Tolls*; Anna Wulf in Doris Lessing's *The Golden Notebook*). But Bradbury, having no character(s) involved in all the action, achieves continuity and unity mainly through his 1) setting, working out the fate of several groups united by their common experience in exotic new locales (Space and Mars); and through his 2) main themes, which are sounded repeatedly in chapter after interchapter (see our Chapter 3, "Bradbury's Themes in *The Martian Chronicles*").

However, Bradbury does establish some of his minor linkage through characters who reappear in a later story, or are at least discussed in a later story after their one appearance. Notice the effects of linkage Bradbury achieves by first introducing Wilder, Hathaway, Parkhill, and Spender in —And the Moon Be Still as Bright, and then having the first two reappear, and the other two discussed, in "The Long Years;" by having Parkhill back again in "The Off Season;" by having Gripp of "The Silent Towns" also discussed in "Years."

Some critics, e.g., Wayne Johnson in *Ray Bradbury*, say that only three characters appear in more than one chapter. They overlook the reappearance of a minor character who nevertheless has great symbolic significance in two of the interchapters: the luggage store man, the fourth character to be on stage twice.

CONTRASTS

Like the musician and the painter, Bradbury achieves many of his best effects through the use of vivid contrasts. His descriptions, for example, are often compounded of sharp, definite details mixed with hazy suggestions. He will go from the lush style of "Ylla" to the lean style of "The Earth Men" back to the rich language of "The Third Expedition." He will treat the same theme—e.g., What happens to the person left behind?—in a comic manner ("The Silent Towns"), then in a tragic mode ("The Long Years"). His settings, sometimes explicitly, contrast the Martians' love of permanent beauty and harmony with the Americans' willingness to settle for temporary utility. His characterizations especially are enhanced by contrasts: for instance, between Walter Gripp's fantasy-expectations of Genevieve and his real experience with her; between the Martians as Parkhill sees them and his wife and the reader see them; between

Parkhill's closed attitudes toward the Martians and Gomez's openness. In Chapter 5, "Chapter-by-Chapter Textual Analysis," we shall explore the artistic effects Bradbury achieves with his continual, contrapuntal comparisons.

SUSPENSE

Literary structure—form, as we suggested earlier—may be defined as the way an author excites our curiosity and then satisfies it. Between posing questions and answering them, he tries to keep us in a constant state of suspense, of uncertainty about the outcome of the conflicts he has set in motion. Since Bradbury is a master of suspense, you will find it profitable to analyze his techniques for keeping us on edge. Note, for instance, that he does not let us actually see an astronaut from Earth until the fourth chronicle. Keeping main characters off-stage until the action is well advanced is one standard trick for building suspense. Another trick is to have a main character disappear, as do Spender in "—And the Moon Be Still as Bright" and Tom in "The Martian." But Bradbury goes beyond such standard tricks to plant new questions in our minds paragraph by paragraph. You will find good examples in "The Long Years." Why does Hathaway's family answer his questions "neatly"? Why is their debate about Earth's fate a "silent" debate? Why, when Hathaway calls for a toast, does the wine run down the chins of four of the five Hathaways? Usually, all such questions are resolved by a story's end. But an appreciation of the characters' predicament, of their courage in facing uncertainties, often requires that some questions be left hanging. In "The Million-Year Picnic," the last chapter, Dad is obviously worried about whether "the evil men" will pursue his family to Mars. We'll never know. They would not be true-to-life characters if they weren't facing new problems even at book's end.

SUSPENSE: HYPOTHESIZING

Much of Bradbury's suspense is dependent on a major characteristic of SF: Its heroes are constantly trying to reason out what is happening, what they have to do next. The narrator in Jules Verne's *Twenty Thousand Leagues Under the Sea* and in H. G. Wells's *The War of the Worlds* invoke all their scientific knowledge to hypothesize about their predicaments. Their hypothesis virtually outline the later action and—since only one hypothesis will prove to be true—create curiosity about which one will explain everything. Bradbury's Captains Williams, Black, and Wilder thus contribute to our state of suspense in the *Chronicles*.

POINT OF VIEW

A major narrative technique is one we call literary point of view. An author must decide who will tell his story. In his 1985 mystery novel, *Death is a Lonely Business*, Bradbury allows his hero to tell his own story in the first person (I, we). An advantage of the character-as-narrator "I" point of view is that the reader can better identify with, actually get inside, one character; we see and hear all the action through his or her eyes and ears. What may be a disadvantage, of course, is that we can know only what he or she knows, or thinks he or she knows. But this may increase the suspense; what do other people know that the narrator does not? Or it may decrease the suspense: since the narrator is telling the story, we know from the start that he has survived everything.

Bradbury never uses the first-person point-of-view in the *Chronicles*. Instead he always has the author telling the story in the third-person (he, she, they). But he does use several variations of this approach.

AUTHOR OMNISCIENT

In all twelve interchapters, and in one chapter—"There Will Come Soft Rains"—Bradbury is the omniscient narrator. He uses all the godlike powers granted to the storyteller by time-honored tradition. He can stand far above his creation and give us an overall view or he can zoom in for a closeup. He can take us back and forth across time and space, and show how distant events are related. And he can editorialize as he sees fit, speaking in his own, godlike, authorial voice. Advantage: the reader knows more than any or all characters know. This provides us with ironic situations (about which more soon will follow) and gives the reader a sense of transcendence over all situations.

AUTHOR AS LIMITED NARRATOR

The author may choose to speak in the third person but to limit our perception to what one character knows. In several chapters (e.g., "Ylla") Bradbury limits his world view to one character's perception throughout the action. In other stories (e.g., "—And the Moon Be Still as Bright"), he shifts the point of view from one character's to another's. In still other stories (e.g., "The Long Year's"), he shifts from one character's viewpoint to another's and then to that of the author omniscient.

The advantage of Bradbury's use of flexible point-of-view is that he combines some of the objectivity of the author omniscient with some of the subjectivity of the first-person narrator. To aid you in your study of one of the most fascinating techniques in fictional narration, we shall comment frequently on literary point-of-view in Chapter 5, "Chapter-by-Chapter Textual Analysis."

SETTING

It plays a major role in SF. The SF aficionado wants avidly to read about new and exotic places, both for an understanding of how living beings there interact with their natural environment and for what their artificial environment reveals about them. Always implicit in SF settings is a contrast in goals and achievements with humanity's settings on Earth.

Bradbury's Mars, as we have seen in Chapter 2, is based partly on the Mars imagined by astronomers like Percival Lowell and partly on Bradbury's love of classical Greek environments. Thus, Bradbury's Mars is a dust-stormy desert whose engineers have fought global drought with a magnificent network of canals; they have built grace and charm into their machinery; their architects have striven for permanent beauty in their habitats; Martian technologies all harmonize with Nature.

Bradbury uses Mars, then, as a landscape where Americans can reenact for us their savage mistreatment of new territories, their callous contentment with temporary architecture and mechanisms that stress utility at the expense of esthetics. He is drawing a lesson for us when he makes an American town on Mars look like a frontier village in the Old West, or like any one of hundreds of identical drab cities in America today. Bradbury's settlers on Mars learn nothing from the natural and artificial settings on the Mars they despoil.

As we shall see, setting is so important to Bradbury that it will not only tell us something about his characters, it will even sometimes become a character itself, as in "Usher II" and "There Will Come Soft Rains."

LITERARY ALLUSIONS

Bradbury uses quotations from, and allusions to, more than a dozen classical authors to help him establish his situations and themes. His story "There Will Come Soft Rains" serves, among other things, as a sequel to Sara Teasdale's poem of the same name. A Ben Jonson song, not to mention a nursery rhyme, introduces Freudian imagery relevant to the psychological state of certain Martians. A poem by Lord Byron both helps to establish the mood of a setting and to give it meaning. Situations from Edgar Allan Poe, Lewis Carroll, and the Brothers Grimm help Bradbury make his point about the reaction of imagination when it is repressed by cold logic. The better versed the reader in classical literature, the richer the texture and the resonance of Bradbury's stories. Our textual analysis (Chapter 5) will help you establish and understand these allusions.

CLASSICAL PARALLELS AND
HISTORICAL ALLUSIONS

Familiarity with classical Greek culture and modern American history can add to the appreciation of the many different dimensions of *Chronicles*. The Martians' golden fruits, fluted columns, marble amphitheaters, villas, cities with fountains in their squares, all make it clear how Spender can reconstruct their philosophy ("—And the Moon Be Still as Bright"). Some scenes in *Chronicles* extend the Greeks' concern with protean natures. And the dialogue between Mr. Ttt and Captain Williams is a good contemporary example of the ancient theatrical device known as *stichomythy* ("The Earth Men").

Just four random examples will suffice to show how Bradbury wants his settlement of Mars both to recapitulate and to comment on the white man's settlement of America. Bradbury's settlers treat the Martians, we learn, as the white man has treated the Indian; and they plan to build up Mars as they built the West, in part, by exploiting Chinese and Mexican labor. His settlers also continue the good side of the American character by extending both the Johnny Appleseed project and the "Underground Railway" to the "Red Planet."

CHARACTERIZATION

One of the reasons we read fiction is to broaden our understanding of people, including, of course, ourselves. We expect then that an author will characterize the people in his story. By this we mean he will at least delineate each person as different from the others. But we hope too for the best the and most we can expect from characterization, namely that at least one person in a story will change in some significant way-significant both for that person and the reader. For when we read, we are all psychologists (and self-analysts) to some degree.

SCOPE OF CHARACTERIZATION

Usually an author requires a full-length novel or drama in which to do justice to his main character(s), to depict the long-range changes in their makeup. Almost by definition, then, we expect that in a short story the fiction-writer may be able to explore well only one aspect of his main character(s), especially if he reveals that aspect or quality in a state of change.

This is an important consideration in discussing characterization in the *Chronicles* because, as we have seen, fourteen of them were originally short stories that have been reworked into novel-chapters. Almost all of the characters, then, have only one chapter in which to reveal their makeup. Only three of the characters in the chapters (Sam Parkhill, Captain Wilder, Hathaway) make a second appearance, and only three (Parkhill, Wilder, and Walter Gripp) are even discussed later in chapters in which they do not reappear.

It would seem that Bradbury has less opportunity for extended, deep, complex characterization in the *Chronicles* than he enjoys in *Fahrenheit 451*, in which his hero, Guy Montag, has an entire book in which to learn, grow, suffer, change radically. It is quite a surprise to realize that in spite of the limitations of the *Chronicles'* short-story-chapter form, Bradbury manages here to create several fairly complex characters and about a dozen highly memorable ones. It remains significant that the most thoroughly developed characters are those who appear in the longest story ("—And the Moon Be Still as Bright") and reappear later (Wilder and Hathaway in "The Long Years" and Parkhill in "The Off Season").

ROUND AND FLAT CHARACTERS

Persons in fiction who are deeply characterized are called (since the novelist E. M. Forster so called them) "round" characters. We can see them from all sides. They are represented as highly organized complexes of traits, qualities, needs, flaws, virtues; they are capable of surprising us "in a convincing way" because of their complexity. In our textual analysis, we shall discover that Captain Wilder, Spender, Ylla, and Governor Dad, and a few others are the closest we can come to round characterization in the short-story-chapter format.

Most persons in fiction are not fully characterized. They are called "flat" characters because we can see only one side of them. They are usually minor characters. It is not entirely unfair for an author to treat some characters as flat because even in real life there are many people whom we get to know only in a shallow way. Some flat characters are "types" or "stock characters," traditional familiar figures who appear regularly in the history of literature: the henpecked husband, the braggart soldier, the hardboiled private eye. Needless to say, flat characters have no chance to grow or even change much, and their behavior is always by definition predictable. Flat characters in *Chronicles* include Pop the gas-station man ("Night Meeting") and Cherokee in "—And the Moon Be Still as Bright." Also types, as well as flat, are Yll the jealous husband ("Ylla"), Parkhill the greedy braggart-bully ("—And the Moon Be Still as Bright" and "The Off Season"), and Garrett the suave, sadistic administrator ("Usher II").

CHORUS CHARACTERS

Some characters seem to exist mainly to state the author's views. They are called "chorus characters" because in ancient drama the ideas expressed by the chorus were assumed to be the author's own. Two examples in *Chronicles* are "The Taxpayer" in the interchapter of that name and Pop in "Night Meeting." Dad in "The Million-Year Picnic" and Spender in "—And the Moon Be Still as Bright" could be considered chorus characters except that they are too fully developed to be so categorized.

FOILS

Jewelers will often place a sheet of foil behind a gem to enhance it, to bring out its qualities. The fiction writer often uses one character as a foil for another. Elma in "The Off Season" is calm in the presence of the Martians, serving as a perfect foil for panicky Sam Parkhill. Because he is a contrast to the main character, the foil will sometimes trigger the action. Thus, Biggs in "—And the Moon Be Still as Bright" pollutes the environment and causes a violent reaction in Spender, who respects Nature and wants to preserve the Martian landscape.

GROUP CHARACTERIZATIONS

Conflict in fiction necessarily involves not only individuals with different needs and means, but also groups with different goals, ideals, and values. In the *Chronicles*, we become aware that Spender groups most Americans as unwilling to learn anything from other cultures, as interested only in exploiting other peoples, as indifferent to beauty and life as its own excuse for being, while he characterizes the Martians as the exact opposite in every respect. Dad in "The Million-Year Picnic" characterizes as one group "the evil men," the people who developed science too quickly, who used it mainly for wars and greedy colonization, the people who exiled Wilder, harassed Stendhal and Pikes, and set American policy on Mars. Dissenters like The Taxpayer, Dad, Spender, and Wilder are obviously a much smaller group than the conformists like Parkhill, Garrett, Teece, Biggs, and Spaulding, but we are always made aware of the fact that the two sides do act as identifiable groups, and in that sense, as types.

BRADBURY'S METHODS OF CHARACTERIZATION

There are four main methods a writer can use to characterize a person in his fiction. He can offer his own description and judgment of that character. He can report images and impressions of the character held by the other characters. He can report the character's own private estimates of him- or herself. And the author can have the character publicly reveal his or her own nature through his or her speech and behavior. In the *Chronicles*, Bradbury uses all four techniques.

AUTHORIAL DESCRIPTION

In his chapters (short stories), Bradbury the author almost never intrudes. But in his interchapters, in which he gives us overviews of the interplanetary situation, he uses his privilege as author omniscient to describe and judge each wave of settlers directly, in his own voice. Thus in "The Locusts," he characterizes them as eager to wipe out everything not American on Mars. In "The Naming of Names" he satirizes those professionals too timid to come until the planet was made safe, and now ready to run the lives of people more adventurous than themselves. He editorializes freely: " . . . it was inevitable that some of these people would push back." And in "The Shore," he notes that there should have been settlers on Mars "from other countries with other accents and other ideas," but the Americans intended to keep Mars American (as their colony).

TAG NAMES

Practically the only way that Bradbury offers authorial judgment in the short-story chapters is in his occasional use of tag names. The most prominent examples are in "Usher II," where William Stendhal, Mr. Garrett, and Mr. Pikes all bear names that are judgments of their characters. In the interchapter "The Luggage Store," Father Peregrine is also characterized by name. This technique will be explored in detail in our Chapter 5, "Chapter-by-Chapter Textual Analysis."

DEFINITION BY OTHER CHARACTERS

Bradbury makes maximum artistic use of the possibilities of characterizing a person through the impressions he has made on others. Practically all we know about Pikes in "Usher II" we learn from Stendhal's colorful reflections on the career of his colleague. Ylla's rueful thoughts on marriage in general and her husband in particular prepare us well to understand his behavior. It's Spender's opinion of Cherokee in "—And the Moon Be Still as Bright" that helps make the Indian's brief appearance so meaningful and his death so meaningless. It's Wilder's order not to shoot Spender in the head that sums up Walker's and the reader's respect for Spender as a thinker. Notice how succinctly Bradbury characterizes both Wilder and Spender by having them look across open space at each other and ponder each other. And how delicious it is for us to observe how Mom and Dad act in "The Million-Year Picnic" unaware that Timothy is beginning to think about just how parents do run things!

CHARACTER SELF-EVALUATION

Bradbury's favorite point of view in the chapters is that of the author as limited narrator-limited, that is, to the perceptions of one character. One advantage of this viewpoint is that it includes the character's perceptions of himself. Whether these self-evaluations are objective or not, they still give us important clues to the character's nature, conflicts, and weaknesses. In "Ylla," it's her reverie that tells us that she is starved for love. In "—And the Moon Be Still as Bright," it's Wilder's introspection that tells us he'd like to be more like Spender in ideals but unlike him in emotions. Perhaps the best use of a person's self-evaluation as a means of characterization occurs in "The Million-Year Picnic." Bradbury tells the story from the point of view of Timothy, the oldest of three boys. Through his tight self-control, we learn that he now feels on the side of the adults, his parents, in helping them to handle the younger boy's psychological problems on Mars; and now feels like being a little boy himself, free to cry over his own childish fears.

It is significant that in "Way in the Middle of the Air" and "The Off Season" Bradbury takes us inside nobody. Although the action in these stories centers around, respectively, Mr. Teece and Sam Parkhill, we know nothing of their inner life as we do of Ylla's, Wilder,'s Timothy's. The implication, by contrast, is masterful. Teece and Parkhill are exactly the kind of persons about whom we feel there is nothing spiritual going on anyway. They are, by default, characterized as incapable of self-analysis.

CHARACTERIZATION THROUGH ACTION

But these methods of characterization—description of a person by the author, by other characters, and by himself—become most effective only when they are augmented by that person's self-revelation through his actions and dialogue. As Henry James made clear, action and characterization are ultimately identical. Action tests character; character initiates action. Notice how variously Bradbury uses the landings by Earth men to test the character of the Martians. Yll ("Ylla") reveals himself as so narrow in cosmic view that he will allow his own insecurity as a husband to terminate the chance of interplanetary association. Mr. Xxx ("The Earth Men") shows us how people can be tragically limited in their perception of events by their experience with earlier events. Tom ("The Martian") is so desperately lonely that he risks his life by taking on human roles just to enjoy human company. And when the Martians ("The Off Season") act as a race, in unison, out of their official policy, they prove to be incapable of violence, showing their superiority of character by turning the other cheek.

EARTH MEN TESTED: FOUND GOOD

Equally instructive is the way Bradbury uses the Mars landings as a test of character as it is produced on Earth. The captains—Williams, Black, and Wilder—all prove to be deserving of their rank because of their superior intellect. (This in itself is a prime example of how SF can be utopian in its aims.) Williams and Black prove to be able to reason out what kind of trap they're in, an intellectual feat in both cases. Wilder, faced with a mutiny by his archaeologist, is able to learn from the mutineer before he executes him. And before he dies, Spender, the one-man-mutiny (note that he had hoped to recruit both Cherokee and Wilder to his view), is able to give his captain a brilliant analysis of a major problem in interplanetary exploration. His tragedy is that he has not had the emotional control needed to carry out his intellectual judgments in a more realistic way.

Wilder emerges, then, as Bradbury's ideal character, with a workable blend of feelings and intelligence. When we meet him twenty years later, he is still the superb democratic leader, in easy, casual control of the situation, open to suggestions from others, impartial (remember how he could sympathize even with Biggs?) But note that this ideal leader has been kicked upstairs.

EARTH MEN TESTED: FOUND BAD

The people that Bradbury has tested in action and found virtuous—like Gomez ("Night Meeting"), Driscoll ("The Green Morning"), and Lafe ("The Martian")—are far outnumbered by the people Dad ("The Million-Year Picnic") calls "the evil men." These people also prove themselves by their action and their dialogue. It suffices to mention only three here, three of Bradbury's superb portraits of evil: Teece the racist who, if he loses his black targets, will surely find white ones; Parkhill whose actions and dishonest speech typify the low grasping mentality that can see in Mars only a place to practice greed and to settle all problems with a gun; and Garrett the cynical bureaucrat whose energy can go entirely into originality of style because his ideas are originated for him by his superiors. These "evil men" are supported by the hordes of nameless ones who ravaged the natural and human resources of the American West, Alaska, Puerto Rico, and finally Mars.

LITERARY STYLE DEFINED

In the broadest sense of the word, an author's style refers to the ways in which he structures his plot, creates character, implants his themes, and uses language. In that broad sense, then, we have so far been talking about the first three elements of Bradbury's style. But in the narrowest sense of the word, style refers only to an author's own characteristic way with words, the way he achieves his original texture and quality of language.

In that sense, then, we come only now to a discussion of Bradbury's style. Here we are interested in his diction (choice of words), his use of words to represent revealing, sensuous details, his success in making evocative comparison (through metaphor, simile, symbol), his use of that resonating figure of speech known as irony, his characteristic sentence maneuvers, his success with dialogue, the way he draws on the techniques of black humor, and his tone.

DICTION

In his authoritative four-volume anthology, *The Road to Science Fiction*, James Gunn calls Bradbury "a writer drunk on words, and with those magic words he has created dreams for readers that seemed better than reality." The magic begins in Bradbury's very choice of words. He surprises us again and again with the way he puts usual words to unusual uses, and thinks of unusual words with which to make the usual more noticeable. For example, preening is a bird's action in cleaning its feathers with its beak or bill. But in "The Off Season," the word describes the way the sharp prows of the Martian sail-boats move over the sand. A word for glossy black is raven, because of that bird's color. But when Bradbury uses the word in "Usher II" to denote raven grass, the word changes not only the color of the grass but also the shape of its blades: they become feathery. When Sam ("The Off Season") pumps bullets into Martian buildings, Bradbury calls the resulting fragments not splinters or bits but flinders. He exploits both the general and specialized, craft meaning of many words. Sam sneers at his old comrades still soldiering, meaning both that they are still in the service and still goldbricking on the job. Bradbury does not hesitate to use a word labeled "regional" in the dictionary if he can make its meaning clear in context: Thus, in "The Green Morning" rain *mizzled* down out of the high air. Note that while air is high (several miles high on earth), how often have we heard it described that way? Needless to say, in Bradbury's word-magic, frost and frosty things always become more unusual: *rime* and *rimed.*

SENSUOUS DETAIL

We can feel the fine mist on our faces when Bradbury says it mizzled; feel the feathery quality of the blades of raven grass. With Bradbury, diction is the search for words that appeal to the senses as well as to the mind. We can hear what happened when Mr. Xxx tapped the spaceship ("The Earth Men") and the rocket gonged. Bradbury even makes us realize we can *smell . . . lathed brass* ("Usher II"). Most often he makes us connect with things through more than one of our senses. We see and hear as Biggs's body drifts with slow unconcern and makes a hollow bubbling sound ("—And the Moon Be Still as Bright"). We can see and feel the drumsticks sucked clean that lay brittle on the plates ("The Third Expedition").

EVOCATIVE COMPARISONS

When Bradbury uses *preening* to describe the action of his sandships, he implicitly compares their sharp prows with the beaks of birds. Such an implicit comparison—called a metaphor—shocks us by forcing us to assimilate a similarity between dissimilars. This shock makes the action more emotional for us and helps us achieve the desired vicarious experience of the characters' emotional states. When Bradbury says Ylla was washed up on the shore of awakening, he is conjuring up an exciting analogy between sleep and floating in a liquid element, and between awakening and landing on a solid element. In "Way in the Middle of the Sky" he calls the blacks' ascending rockets golden bobbins, a fine comparison of their ships' shape with that of spools, with of course, a hint that they are threading their way through space.

SIMILES
Bradbury has a great fondness for and an unending supply of similes, metaphors in which the comparison is made explicit by the use of the equal signs *like* or *as*. What a shock of recognition we feel when we read that Bluebeard ("Usher II") has whiskers like acetylene flame . . . that bright blue-and-yellow sparkling that welders use! What a reminder of our mortality it is to read that Hathaway's drifting through rooms of dead Martians is like walking in a pile of autumn leaves. How Bradbury catches the psychological violence of censorship when he says they seized Pikes' films like entrails from the camera. Indeed, it's a rare page of the *Chronicles* that doesn't excite us with at least one brilliant simile.

EXTENDED SIMILES
Bradbury enjoys two kinds of extended similes, both of them rare in today's literature: 1) The multiple simile, such as he uses when he describes the effects a Martian woman has on Sam with a series of nine similes; 2) The Homeric (epic) simile, in which experience A is likened to experience B, which is then described at length (a long digression actually) to explore the full feelings involved. Waiting for the big event to burst on her, Ylla compares her wait with protracted expectations of storm—a 150-word simile Homer himself might envy!

SYMBOLISM AND ALLEGORY
Bradbury's poetic mind produces, too, many examples of the ultimate metaphor-symbols. A symbol is something that stands for something else larger than itself; usually it's a material thing or specific action that stands for something immaterial or general. We've already seen how Wilder's wanting Spender shot not through the head symbolizes Wilder's desire to keep Spender's ideas intact and viable. And in "The Million-Year Picnic" the family goes on a fishing trip and then does not fish—or do they? Actually the boys are fishing for the full truth, the parents for the right word and occasion for risking the

truth; they're all fishing for clues to their own feelings—while hunting for a new homesite. The one real fish they do see is seen by Dad as symbolic of war! In "Chapter-by-Chapter Textual Analysis," Chapter 5, we shall discuss other symbols, including an instance of extended symbolism that becomes allegory.

IRONY

That Bradbury is always in perfect and playful control of his subject is evident from his easy use of irony, a figure of speech not easily mastered by most writers. The word *irony* covers all the many ways an author can play on the differences between appearance and reality. What we call *verbal irony,* or saying one thing and meaning another, is recognizable to us in its simplest form as sarcasm. Thus Yll says to Ylla: "I never thought you were a nature lover, but you're certainly interested in the sky tonight." He really means, of course that she's interested in the sky because of another kind of love. What we call *dramatic irony* occurs when we watch how characters act in ignorance of facts that we happen to know. Thus, in "The Earth Men," Captain Williams declares the fate of the First Expedition to be unknown, a fate that is, however, well-known to the reader. Bradbury especially revels in *irony of situation,* that is, developments that are the exact opposite of what was expected or intended. In "The Third Expedition," Captain Black is angry at his men for being lured away from their duty; ironically, he is soon lured away himself. "Usher II" is a carnival of ironic situations. Stendhal thinks he has killed the real Garrett, but Pikes discovers that they've only destroyed Garrett's robot of himself. However, this only foreshadows a more complicated version of the same kind of ironic reversal. Garrett and others think real persons have been killed; they accept Stendhal's statement that only their look-alike robots have been destroyed, yet all the while it is the real people being killed while their robots remain as proof that the real people are still alive!

The greatest irony of situation is—as we've pointed out in our study of the plot—that the Americans intended to settle permanently on Mars but then instead return to the aid of their native country only to be destroyed there in a nuclear war they could have avoided by staying on Mars.

SENTENCE MANEUVERS

In 1950, when Bradbury published the *Chronicles*, most of the literary (and advertising) world stood in great awe of the Great American Stylist, Ernest Hemingway. Editors advised writers, and teachers forced students to follow Hemingway's lead, that is, to use very few adjectives and many short and simple sentences. But Bradbury violated these sacred prescripts and still produced effective, literary, and popular prose that often sounds like poetry. (To top it off, he ridicules Hemingway's "realism" in "Usher II.") For example, his one hundred-word interchapter "The Old Ones" contains 13 one-word adjectives! It consists of two long sentences, the first forty words, the other sixty. How does Bradbury succeed in lightening the dead weight of adjectives? In several ways. He makes sure the adjectives, as we've seen in our discussion of his diction-and-details, are striking adjectives: the old people are (to choose just two examples) *dried-apricot* people, *mummy* people. Furthermore, Bradbury counter-balances the thirteen adjectives with nine action words, verbs and verb particles, each describing a striking activity: e.g., *feeling their pulses and spooning syrups . . .* Then, the two sentences are very rhythmical in their organization, each with its own kind of *parallelism*, Walt Whitman's (and the Psalmists') favorite device for musical effects. The first contains four parallel phrases; the second, two parallel clauses. And the two sentences are exact contrasts in type. The first is a loose sentence (one in which the main idea is expressed early and is followed by subsidiary ideas). The second is a periodic sentence (the main idea is held till last, near the period). Finally, the music is capped with significant repetitions: the piece opens with the idea that at last, the old people *come to* Mars, and closes with *came at last to* Mars. The word people is sounded six times. And there are scores of such prose poems in *Chronicles*. They, of course, alternate with leaner, swifter passages, but they form one basis for Bradbury's reputation as a stylist.

DIALOGUE

Another basis for his stature as a stylist is his easy control of dialogue that more than meets the four basic requirements of this element of fiction:

1. We want each character to talk differently from the way the author writes.

2. We want each character to have his or her own unique manner of verbal expression consonant with his or her nature and circumstances.

3. We expect that dialogue will figure significantly in pacing the action.

4. We look to the dialogue to play a major part in developing character.

Bradbury's opening story immediately accustoms us to this high level of dialogue. The author sets the scene and sketches in the domestic situation in his typical prose: slow poetic paragraphs alternating with short fast dramatic ones. When the dialogue begins, Ylla's speech is personal, candid, dreamy, questioning, moody; her husband's comprises impersonal, reserved, factual, mainly self-assured answers. Later, when he begins to take the situation more seriously, his speeches become for a while more conciliatory, hypocritically tender, more questioning. Finally, though, his is the demanding, commanding, even angry or contemptuous voice of the man-in-control; hers becomes at last the hysterical speech of the woman-under-control and frustrated.

See how concentrating on the dialogue shows how central it is: describing the quality of the characters' speeches is actually a way of summarizing the story. If you decide—in a paper or report—to make a study of Bradbury's dialogue, extend our observations here into the conversations between Lafe and Tom ("The Martian"); Sam and Elma ("The Off Season"); Gomez and Ca ("Night Meeting"); Spender and Wilder

("—And the Moon Be Still as Bright"); and into others that also seem especially artistic to you.

BLACK HUMOR
Long used in combination with other techniques, black humor became the dominant mode in many works of fiction in the 1960s. This is an extreme kind of humor, deliberately used on tragic subjects, that makes us laugh so that we may postpone crying. In other words, by so tempering and postponing our bitter weeping the author manages to take us even closer to his tragic material and tragic message. Shakespeare uses black humor as a minor technique, a mere side-effect, when he has the mortally wounded Mercutio say such things to Romeo as "Seek me tomorrow and you will find me a grave man." Joseph Heller, in contrast, uses black humor as the major technique, the main attraction, in *Catch-22*, published in 1961.

Bradbury may then be considered a pioneer in the use of black humor as the all-pervasive mode in a work of fiction. For his "The Earth Men"—in which real astronauts, expecting to be treated as heroes when they land on Mars, are instead treated as Martians posing as Earth men—was written in 1948. So it qualifies as one of the first genuine black-humor stories of the contemporary kind. A better example of Bradbury's humor is "There Will Come Soft Rains." Much as the atomic devastation of America makes us want to weep, we can't help laughing at such comic details as a cigar stand that, at the same time each day, produces a lighted cigar (even when no humans are left alive). But the best example of Bradbury's work in this vein is his savage attack on censorship in "Usher II."

TONE
After this survey of Bradbury's style, and before we embark on our more detailed textual analysis of the *Chronicles*, we should comment on the tone of his novel, that is, the attitude of the author as revealed in his style. Generally speaking, Bradbury becomes subjective in tone, revealing his own attitudes freely, only in the interchapters, where he speaks directly in the authorial voice or through a chorus character. He remains

objective in tone in almost all the story-chapters. However, in black humor as savage as "Usher II," an author can hardly conceal his personal involvement. Bradbury obviously relishes Stendhal's revenge on those who censor books. It's Bradbury's own revenge.

TEXTUAL ANALYSIS
MARTIAN CHRONICLES: PART I

TITLE AND CHRONOLOGY

In linking the words Martian and Chronicles in his title, Bradbury expects to stir up interest and suspense. A chronicle is an official—often a sacred—register of events set down as they happen. The prototypes are the records kept by the Biblical kings David and Solomon, later the separate annals of the kingdoms of Israel and Judah, and then the post-exilic First and Second Books of the *Chronicles*. The most famous post-Biblical work is the *Anglo-Saxon Chronicle*, which contains year-by-year entries of happenings in the English kingdoms from the start of the Christian Era to the year 1154.

What can it mean then when an author offers us such chronicles about Mars the "Red Planet," the planet that's been the main focus of our concern about extraterrestrial life and the one nearby planet that scientists regard as suitable for human habitation?

Bradbury sounds another innovative note when he heads his list of chapter titles, keyed to page numbers, not the table of contents but "Chronology." Thus, he immediately reminds us of the relationship between chronicles and chronology. And so he also apprises us of the futuristic nature of the *Chronicles*, dating them from the penultimate year of the twentieth century (1999) through the first quarter of the next (2026). Then, with his chapter titles, Bradbury also introduces the basic technique of fantasy: he offers enough of the familiar ("The Summer Night," "The Luggage Store") to make the unfamiliar more credible ("Rocket Summer," "Ylla").

JANUARY 1999: ROCKET SUMMER

TITLE

In tune with the futuristic nature of his story, Bradbury begins with a *neologism* (a newly invented word or old words used with new meanings). We may know what *rocket* and *summer* mean as separate words, but not what they signify when coupled. Drawing on the analogy of Indian Summer, a period of warm weather after the first frosts of autumn, Bradbury creates the phrase Rocket Summer to define the unseasonal heat blasted over Ohio in mid winter by the exhausts of departing spaceships. That the rocket made climates suggests other meanings: there are social and psychological climates as well as meteorological ones.

STRUCTURAL FUNCTION
This brief sketch—a kind of Currier-and-Ives picture of the effect of rocket launchings on nearby small-town life—is one of several sketches Bradbury created to link some fourteen short stories about Mars into a novel. This one serves as prelude to all the *Chronicles*; others serve as interludes, interchapters, or bridges between major stories.

POINT OF VIEW
Bradbury narrates his first chronicle from the point of view of the author omniscient, able to observe anyone, anything, anywhere.

STYLE
Even this one-page vignette can serve as a full introduction to Bradbury's famous style. He achieves a rapid, dramatic contrast between natural winter and artificial summer by piling up vivid details (icicles fringing every roof, falling snow turning to hot rain) and using colorful verbs (the chicken *worked off* their winter clothes, the heat *pulsed*). Even in this five-paragraph curtain raiser, we can sense Bradbury's love of metaphor when he first pictures the housewives bundled in their furs as *lumbering like great black bears* and then as *shedding their bear disguises.*

SCIENCE, FICTION, FACT, AND "ROCKET SUMMER"
When the *Chronicles* appeared in 1950, rocket ships were still just science fiction, but they were well grounded in scientific theory. The Russian Konstantin Tsiolkovsky (1857–1935) had

already laid down the mathematical theory for rocket propulsion, and the German Hermann Oberth had pioneered in rocketry experiments. Both said they were inspired by Jules Verne's design of rockets as retrojets in his early SF classic, *From the Earth to the Moon* (1865). And the American Robert Hutchings Goddard (1882–1945) had already built the grandfathers of the Space Age rockets. He described himself as inspired by the SF of H. G. Wells.

It was Verne who had first speculated on the effects of launching a spaceship on the environment. As his space capsule "blast off," an "immense geyser of flame" shot up as the ship cleaved the air "through clouds of blazing vapor." Result: "Not one spectator remained standing. . . ." The climate was affected, darkly, for days after.

Bradbury's speculation also stresses the heat generated, but with a less drastic, yet more dramatic effect on the people nearby.

By 1969, nineteen years after Bradbury's speculation, rocket launchings proved to have no such widespread or sustained effect on the temperature in the general area of the takeoff. There was, however, something like the pulsing that Bradbury had visualized. The *New York Times* said that the launching of the Apollo 11 moonshot "sent a tremor through the ground and staccato shock waves beating at an estimated . . . one million" spectators.

FEBRUARY 1999: YLLA

CONFLICT

To represent life at its most dynamic, the fiction writer must discover and develop the conflicts inherent in the situation he depicts. In "Ylla," Bradbury's first full story in *Chronicles*, he displays his talent for handling conflict in all its variations.

1. *Conflict between individuals*—Between Ylla, a telepathic Martian housewife who dreams of the arrival of a

spaceship from Earth, and Yll, her jealous husband who intends to keep her from meeting Earth men.

2. *Conflict between groups*—Between native Martians, as represented by Yll, and strangers from earth, by Nathaniel York and Bert.

3. *Conflict within the individual*—Within Ylla, her desire to meet York and her duty to obey her husband.

4. *Conflict between ideas*—Between male supremacy and female resistance; between the work ethic and imagination; between the Earth men's mores and Martian mores.

POINT OF VIEW
Bradbury tells this story in the third person (he, she, they) from the point of view of Ylla. Technically, this means that we, as readers, can know and experience only what Ylla knows and experiences. In effect, all of the action is staged for us in her consciousness. Yll is onstage only when she sees him; he is offstage when she can only hear him. We can imagine offstage action only through her sense of sound and her telepathic perceptions.

SCIENCE FICTION
The central event in this story, of course, is the arrival of a rocketship from Earth, as we infer from Ylla's seeing its glint in the sky and hearing its great roar. Presumably, this is the rocket launched a few weeks before in "Rocket Summer," later to be referred to as "the First Expedition." A second crucial SF feature is the revelation that—as Schiaparelli and Lowell had hypothesized (Chapter 2)—the Martians have indeed built a network of canals.

But Mars landings and Lowellian canals were, back in 1950, longstanding assumptions in SF. Where Bradbury shows originality in SF is in the many other examples of Martian technology he unveils, several of them prophetic of subsequent developments on Earth. Yll's metal book, which gives forth the voice of a storyteller, seems analogous to our present-day cassette player, which can play back the recited texts of books. Ylla's fog bed, or silent river, which buoys her up when she sleeps, resembles today's water bed. The magnetic dust with which she cleans seems to be a forerunner of our chemically treated dust rags and dust sprays. The Ks' house, with its flowerlike ability to open, turn, or close according to the position of the sun, sounds like a more advanced use of solar energy than we yet have.

Notice that Bradbury allows us to work out for ourselves the full implications of some of his SF inventions. For example, we realize that the Ks' cooking over hot lava indicates they can channel that substance from volcano to house just as they "canal" water from the ice caps to other areas.

SF AND A CLASSICAL ALLUSION

Perhaps Bradbury's most impressive innovation is the method the Ks use for supplying themselves with fruit and other plant foods. Prehistoric people were food gatherers, wandering through forest and field, plucking food from tree and bush. Bradbury's Martians are food gatherers indoors, where they grow fruit out of the walls. That these are golden fruits is one of Bradbury's earliest parallels to classical mythology. Remember that Paris (in Greek mythology), told to pick the fairest of three goddesses, awarded the golden apple to Aphrodite, goddess of love. The allusion is exciting here: Ylla is love-starved.

ECHOES OF BISHOP GODWIN

Bradbury's Martian flame birds are reminiscent of the "gansas" that British Bishop Francis Godwin introduced in his pseudonymous *The Man in the Moone: or a Discourse of a Voyage Thither, By Domingo Gonsales the Speedy Messenger*, published in 1638. Gonsales trains twenty-five wild geese to carry a chair into the air; however, it seems that on their migrations they always visit the moon, and so must Gonsales! The flame birds are typical of the several means of locomotion Bradbury imagines into existence. They also typify his Martians' tendency, in all their inventions, to work in close harmony with Nature. As we discover in "The Martian," their machines are often modeled after animal life, so the flame birds are probably machines.

SCIENCE FANTASY: TELEPATHY

Given the present state of humanity and its weakness in authentic communications, Earth's scientists take a dim view of telepathy, the supposed power some minds have to transfer their thoughts (and to read minds) by some means other than the normal sensory channels. Telepathy is nevertheless a staple procedure in much SF about other worlds where, for all we know, creatures do have more sensory channels than the five that have evolved in Earthlings. Father Peregrine, in Bradbury's "Fire Balloons," poses the question: Suppose the Martians have ten senses? (*The Stories of Ray Bradbury*, 1980).

Note that Bradbury, master storyteller, provides some Martians with telepathic powers and others with none. And so Mr. K is furiously jealous of Mrs. K for enjoying this power. Note too that Bradbury makes his story more suspenseful by making us sense for ourselves that Ylla is telepathic before he has her say so.

ECHOES OF BEN JONSON

We have to figure out for ourselves that Nathaniel York, whose image and speech are teleported to Ylla, must have been singing Drink to me only with thine eyes as his spaceship neared her planet. This classic lovesong, called "To Celia" and written by Ben Jonson in 1616, continues:

> And I will pledge with mine;
> Or leave a kiss but in the cup,
> And I'll not look for wine.

However, Ylla substitutes *within* for *but*, and *ask* for *look*. Is Bradbury suggesting that Ylla's mind is editing or otherwise affecting the messages she is receiving? She does seem to be imposing her own (unconscious?) desires to be taken away from Yll on the visual and verbal impressions she registers from York and his rocket.

Note the relevance of Jonson's song—about eyes, a kiss, the cup—to Ylla's state of mind. A golden-eyed Martian, she is entranced by the fact that Nathaniel's eyes are blue, unheard of on Mars (and therefore, according to her unimaginative husband, impossible). She dreams that York kisses her. And what is it she chooses to clean during her agitation? An amber glass probably used as winecup. While she is consciously preparing to greet York, she seems unconsciously to sense the truth, because she unintentionally loosens her hold on the glass and it smashes on the floor.

STYLE: SYMBOLISM AND SIMILE

The glass, Ylla's equivalent of Jonson's winecup, has become a symbol of her hopes. And Bradbury has already prepared us to consider some of his imagery sexual. Earlier, Ylla wished that Yll would hold her and stroke her like a little harp. The glass also becomes a Freudian symbol for the female sex organ. When it is shattered, it portends Ylla's breakdown. When Yll—not York—comes through the (triangular!) door, she cannot pick up the pieces.

Bradbury's outpouring of similes adds to our visual and tactile perceptions of Mars, as when he describes the flame birds waiting like a bed of coals. Near the climax, he uses a Homeric (epic) simile, an elaborate comparison between Ylla's mounting expectations and our sensations as we wait for a storm to break. Bradbury is apt, too, in the use of that type of a metaphor that makes its comparisons without the equal sign of like or as: the sleeping Ylla is washed up on the shore of awakening.

STYLE: IRONY

Note Bradbury's use of different kinds of irony. He has Yll say one thing but mean another. "I never thought you were a nature lover, but you're certainly interested in the sky tonight." This is sarcasm, a form of verbal irony. What he really means is: "You're certainly on the lookout for that Earthship tonight . . . you're another kind of lover." Bradbury has Yll say more than he realizes: "You cannot keep secrets from me."

This is *dramatic irony*, a situation in which a character says something that has larger meaning for other characters and the audience. For Ylla, as the reader knows, suspects her husband of doing precisely that: keeping secret from her the real nature of his visits to Xi City.

STYLE: SHARPNESS VERSUS SUGGESTIVENESS

A basic characteristic of Bradbury's style is the tension he sets up in our perceptions between sharply drawn details and vague impressions. We have a definite picture of York: black hair, white skin, blue eyes, six-feet one-inch tall. We have a vague image of the Martians: golden-eyed, brown-skinned— but how tall? Their height is only suggested: since Yll sees York as a grotesque giant, we can only infer that Martians must be much smaller. We get a detailed description of Yll's weaponry, but exactly what are blue phosphorous portraits? A bone town? How does a mist uncorked from a bottle become a Scarf?

Bradbury's alternation between the definite and the suggestive puts the reader halfway between solid reality and velvety fantasy; like Ylla, in an advanced state of reverie in which sensuous perception and intuition work together.

CHARACTERIZATION

Our observations so far permit us these generalizations: Ylla is warm, imaginative, romantic, outgoing, adventurous. This is both symbolized by, and realized in, her telepathic powers. Yll is a cold male chauvinist, withdrawn, bound by facts (as he sees them!), jealous, secretive, hypocritical, a believer in the work ethic as an antidote to "silly dreams." His covert, inaccessible nature is symbolized by his putting on a mask. The approach of an Earth rocket precipitates a crisis in their relationship. At the beginning of the story, she still yearns for him to hold and stroke her like a little harp. Since that now seems out of the question, she becomes ripe for an exciting meeting with Captain York. When Yll destroys the Earth men, he also destroys her peace of mind, maybe even her mental integrity.

We cannot separate the real York from her fantasies. But it seems safe to say he is good-looking, extrovert, adventurous, probably romantic—he's been singing a lovesong. His sidekick, Bert, remains just a name. Irony: the two men, if they have a chance to think about it at all, probably think they're being attacked as invaders. They could have no idea they are being killed out of sexual jealousy.

THEMES AND MESSAGE
We can restate action-and-characterization as a set of ideas.

1. *Metamorphosis*—Four changes are brought about that illustrate the following.

2. *Tragic consequences of short-circuit thinking*—An epoch-making expedition has reached Mars but is abruptly terminated for mean, petty, irrelevant reasons. A Martian woman is excited by new hope and crushed, emotionally at least. Her husband changes from being a merely inactive, unloving person to a murderer of innocent strangers on an historic mission. Their marriage changes from being a merely tolerable relationship to bitter, disastrous, destructive.

3. *The effect of point-of-view on perception of reality*—Because Yll has set ideas about the kind of atmosphere that life needs (Mars's air is mostly carbon dioxide), he has believed that Earth cannot support life at all (its air is mostly oxygen). Because he has set ideas about what people look like (like Martians!), he cannot regard the Earth men as people. Because he is sexually jealous, he cannot see the larger implication of their arrival. And because she is romantic and eager for new experience, Ylla has charged her telepathic picture of the Earth men with her own subjective needs.

4. *Male chauvinism as destructive of male character as well as of female character.*

5. *Imagination as subversive of all repressive systems*—
Like his counterparts on Earth, Yll believes imagination
must be suppressed by teaching the work ethic. Put into
Freudian terms, this is repression of the Id by the Ego.

6. *Machines and gadgetry and their effects on life*—
Mars's technology differs from Earth's in that it stresses
a closer harmony with Nature.

1985 POSTSCRIPT TO "YLLA"

In Bradbury's novel *Death is a Lonely Business* (1985) the narrator—a writer forced by circumstances to become a detective—describes how he once "wrote a tale about a Martian
wife who, lovesick, dreams that an earthman drops from the
sky to take her away. . . ."

AUGUST 1999: THE SUMMER NIGHT

STRUCTURAL FUNCTION

This short-short, written especially for the *Chronicles*, serves
as an interchapter, a bridge, between two major stories, "Ylla"
and "The Earth Men."

TITLE

The name of this interlude contributes to the setting, connoting
as it does a time the populace is likely to be relaxing outdoors.

SETTING

Bradbury further develops the scene as both Lowellian (with
his network of canals a global reality) and classical: to the
golden fruits and fluted pillars we saw in "Ylla," the author
adds marble amphitheaters. Such a Graeco-Roman setting connotes classical harmony, beauty, love of public occasions.

POINT OF VIEW

To tell the story of Ylla, Bradbury limited himself to her point
of view. But to narrate "The Summer Night" he shifts back to
the point of view of the author omniscient, able to observe
anyone, anything, anywhere.

THEME

Again Bradbury's main theme is *metamorphosis,* as the Martian populace undergoes sudden change from serene and secure relaxation to a state of panic and nervous dread.

SCIENCE FANTASY

After our experience with the Ks, we can infer that this mass emotional change is triggered by telepathic impressions of some impending event. Bradbury lets us infer that the source of these messages is, once again, English-speaking people, since one Martian entertainer unwittingly sings

> She walks in beauty, like the night
> Of cloudless climes and starry skies;
> And all that's best of dark and bright
> Meet in her aspect and her eyes . . .

These are the opening lines of "She Walks in Beauty," a poem composed by Lord Byron in 1814. To strengthen our inference, Bradbury has Martian children singing the English nursery-rhyme "Old Mother Hubbard."

IMAGINATION UNDER PATRIARCHY

Bradbury succinctly tells us something about personality in patriarchal, male-chauvinist society. The majority of the Martians who are telepathic are women, children, and performing artists. These are the very people most likely in such a world to preserve their intuitive and imaginative powers.

STYLE: IRONY

Again, the song a Martian unwittingly sings resonates with irony. *She walks in beauty like the night / of cloudless climes and starry skies* could be said on this night of a placid Martian female just before she gets the telepathic message. And "Old Mother Hubbard" sounds ominous, suggesting that the Martian woman might *find her cupboard . . . bare.* Literally, this indicates a depletion of the food supply; symbolically, since the cupboard is also a Freudian image for the vagina, it connotes a barren womb.

STYLE: METAPHOR

Characteristically, Bradbury crowds even this short-short with colorful figures of speech. The opening paragraph alone advances scene and mood with three similes: boats are *delicate as bronze flowers*; rows of houses *curve over the landscape like tranquil snakes*; music *rises like blossom scent.*

STYLE: SUGGESTIVENESS AND SUSPENSE

Without saying it outright, Bradbury has let us infer that more Earth rockets are approaching Mars. Does the nursery rhyme mean there are children aboard? What will be the effect this time of encounters of the third kind?

AUGUST 1999: THE EARTH MEN

TITLE

This story title suggests that the fourth chronicle will give us our first direct experience with astronauts from Earth. In keeping them offstage all this time, Bradbury has made good use of a standard device for building suspense.

STRUCTURAL FUNCTION

Just as "Ylla" unfolds the consequences of the Mars landing of a spaceship launched in "Rocket Summer," so "The Earth Men" relates the result of the touchdown of a ship anticipated in "The Summer Night." The linkage is verified by Captain Williams when he calls his crew "The Second Expedition" and declares the fate of the "First" to be unknown. Dramatic irony: the reader watches how a character acts in his ignorance of facts known to the reader.

HOLOGRAPHY: BRADBURY'S VERSION

In 1947, the Hungarian-British physicist Dennis Gabor worked out the theoretical basis for holography, the science of reproducing three-dimensional images on a flat surface. He worked out a practical method in 1965, and for his research he won a Nobel Prize in 1971. In 1948, however, Bradbury had already published, as a magazine piece, "The Earth Men" in which he conceives of an original process of reproducing three-dimensional images in space. We shall call this process hereafter *telepatho-stereo-holography*, or T-S-H for short. Two versions of it function in this chronicle. In the first, a telepathic Martian male hallucinates and projects his hallucinations so that observers can see the same image he sees—of a naked woman, in three dimensions, that is, in stereo. In the second version, a telepathic Martian female changes the observers' perceptions of herself, so that instead of seeing a brown-skinned, golden-eyed Martian they see a statue, or a pillar, or a walking stick. (More than two decades later, George Lucas would use a similar science-fantasy gimmick in his *Star Wars* films: R2D2 can store and project a three-dimensional image that talks.)

Without Bradbury's version of holography, "The Earth Men" would have been impossible. His plot rests on two ground rules: 1) Martians, like Earth men, consider hallucinations to be insane; 2) but Martians also put in the insane asylum anyone who claims to have come from another planet. Qed: "The Earth Men" are guilty on both counts: 1) Their captain allegedly hallucinates images of a spaceship and crew, then projects these images so that sane Martians must also see them; 2) the captain claims to have come from another planet.

CLASSICAL PARALLELS
Bradbury's T-S-H has its antecedent in ancient mythology. In Homer's *Odyssey* we meet Proteus, who can elude people by changing into a tree, running water, or a lion. It is literally correct, then, to say that Bradbury creates some protean characters.

THEMES
"The Earth Men" is one of Bradbury's most intensive and thorough explanations of two of his favorite themes: *Metamorphosis* as explored in the T-S-H situations ("Biological metamorphosis through psychological imbalance," as psychologist Xxx puts it); and *Point of View as a Distortion of Reality*. Because of their massive previous experience with insane Martians who claim to be natives of other planets, the "sane"

Martians are unprepared to recognize and accredit the Earth men as real.

MONTAIGNE AND BRADBURY

To this second theme we add a corollary, which we can best dub Bradbury's Montaignean theme. Michel de Montaigne (1533–1592), whose informal *Essays* paved the way for modern philosophy, insisted that truth exists in no single faction but only in a composite of all points of view. "The Earth Men" is a brilliant example of the tragic consequences of each side smugly believing it owns the truth. Captain Williams and his crew expect their account of their voyage to be instantly believed and hailed: " . . . it's never been done before!" But the Martians have heard that one before! Even a little Martian girl knows enough to refer the Earth men to the proper bureaucrats. And Xxx (Bradbury's jibe at psychologists: on Earth, X stands for the unknown factor in an equation) is absolutely sure that if he "cures" (kills) Williams, the three crewmen and the rocket will vanish since they are merely projections of Williams's mind. This distortion persists: when the dead bodies and the rocket do not vanish, Xxx can only reason that he has been infected by Williams's disease.

Montaigne's main point—so easy to forget under the pressure of modern life—is that we must never rush to such conclusions but rather postpone judgment until all points of view are explored. "The Earth Men" stands as a masterful dramatization of Montaignean truth.

BRADBURY AS BLACK HUMORIST

It's essentially such a grim story that Bradbury must deliberately have decided to treat it as black humor. This is a technique that makes us laugh so that we won't cry . . . yet. Real astronauts expecting to be hailed by the Martians but being locked up as psychotics is typical black humor: extreme irony of situation. A typical black humor scene is the conversation between Mr. Ttt and Captain Williams, each one talking past the other, in short rapid-fire speeches in which the captain's epoch-making news is silenced by Ttt's irrelevant complaints.

CLASSICAL PARALLELS

This dialogue is an excellent example of what in Greek classical drama is called *stichomythy*: a series of staccato statements made alternately by two characters in a state of intense emotion.

BLACK HUMOR, IRONY, CRISIS

The heroes' welcome the Earth men enjoy in (what proves to be) the nuthouse is typical of the kind of irony that black humor thrives on. In its broadest sense, irony is the exploration of differences between appearance and reality. For a happy while, the Earth men think they are at last being recognized for what they are and have accomplished (appearance). When they realize that these "welcomers" are all psychotics—who look like Martians but insist they are natives of other plants— the Earth men realize they are lost (reality). This is the major turning point in the story, leading inexorably to the smash climax, or the murder of four Earth men and the suicide of the psychologist.

CHARACTERIZATION

No character in "The Earth Men" is as well-developed as Ylla is in the story named after her. Each character in "The Earth Men" is a type playing a role determined by the plot: the irascible housewife, annoyed at being interrupted in her work; the busy administrator annoyed at complaints from an obviously crazy man; the know-it-all psychologist happy to discover the perfect specimen. There are moments when we do feel in the presence of flesh-and-blood characters: e.g., the little girl so wise in the ways of her planet, and the four Earth men when they realize the terrible trap they have flown into. But "The Earth Men" stresses not characterization but a well-oiled plot.

POINT OF VIEW

Bradbury tells the story in his authorial voice but first from the point of view of the Earth men, then from that of the murderer-suicide, finally from that of the author omniscient.

STYLE AND TONE

"The Earth Men" has nothing of the velvety texture of the earlier chronicles, none of their color, their rich poetry, none of their suggestiveness. The language is strictly functional, most of the time only advancing the action, some of the time sprouting into sarcasm or grim satire. The narration becomes especially thin near the end. There is one good simile: Mr. Aaa walks so fast he looks like a pair of wild calipers. There is an occasional sensuous detail: when Xxx taps it, the rocket gonged. The literary differences between this fourth chronicle and the earlier three so surprise Wayne Johnson, in his excellent book *Ray Bradbury*, that he calls "The Earth Men" a "throwback to pulp science fiction."

PART 2

MARCH 2000: THE TAXPAYER

FUNCTION, POINT OF VIEW, SETTING

This interchapter-vignette serves as prelude to "The Third Expedition," just as "Rocket Summer" and "The Summer Night" preluded "Ylla" and "The Earth Men," respectively. As author omniscient Bradbury shifts us back briefly to Earth, to Ohio, the setting of "Rocket Summer." An important aim of this section is to remind us—through the voice of the irate taxpayer— that the fates of the First and Second Expeditions are not known on Earth. *Dramatic Irony*: It gives us a feeling of transcendence over reality to be able to watch how a character acts in his ignorance of facts known to us.

CHORUS CHARACTER

The irate taxpayer demanding his rights (here, the right to join the Third) is a pleasant cartoon stereotype. But his list of reasons for wanting to quit Planet Earth sounds a note of specific protest against contemporary conditions that becomes regular fare in Bradbury. Expectation of "an atomic war . . . in two years" was common at the time he was assembling the *Chroni-*

cles. Note that Bradbury's "chorus character" (a character whose main function is to present the author's views, like the chorus in Greek drama) complains about the military draft, censorship, and government control of art and science . . . in the United States. These, too, were common sentiments in the 1950s as America drifted into McCarthyism. Note that the vignette ends with the protester in the paddy wagon, speeding off to jail just as the astronauts leap off to Mars: This is one of several chronicles expressing Bradbury's sympathy with dissenters.

APRIL 2000: THE THIRD EXPEDITION

TITLE

Comparing the dates given in the six chapter titles so far, we can see that Bradbury conceives (in 1950) of one month or less as the time required for an Earth spaceship to reach Mars. When Nasa sent two Viking spacecraft to Mars (in 1976), the voyage lasted ten months. In *The Stories of Ray Bradbury*, his 1980 collection, this chronicle appears under the title of "Mars in Heaven."

STYLE

Reading the opening paragraphs, we realize we are back in the lush narrative style that characterized the first story, "Ylla," and which was interrupted by the lean style of the second, "The Earth Men." The rocket's journey is described in metaphoric language—on launching, it bloomed out great flowers of heat and color, and it moved into the midnight waters of space like a pale sea leviathan. (Did Bradbury have in mind *Moby Dick* when he wrote that simile?) The first "Martian" house the crew sees in also topped with a metaphor: a duncecap roof. Sensuous detail abounds: they watched Mars swing up under them, and later, drumsticks were sucked clean and lay brittle on the plates. This poetic language is cast in Bradbury's best prose rhythms, with frequent, insistent parallel structure in his words, phrases, and clauses.

IRONY

The story resonates with ironic speeches. Hinkston the archaeologist greets his first glimpse of the fourth planet with an affectionate phrase: "Good old Mars!" It will prove to be "old" in some unexpected ways but certainly not good—for the Earth men. And Captain Black reminds his crew that apparently the York rocket had exploded on arrival, and the Williams ship on the day after it landed. *Dramatic irony.* We who know better watch how the crew acts in their ignorance of the full story. And a major crisis, or turning point, is also achieved with irony: first, Black is angry at the men disobeying orders by abandoning the ship; then, seduced by the same Martian powers as they have been, he himself fails to do his duty "to report the men in."

WHAT GENRE? SF? OR HORROR?

"The Third Expedition" qualifies certainly as science fictionantasy, but specialists in the horror story also claim it as a major work in their genre. A modicum of hard-core SF inheres in the fact that the Third's spaceship is armed with atomic weapons (as nuclear arms were called in 1950); it is big enough to contain several decks ("levels"—a far cry from Verne's one-room space capsule); and its captain has been scientifically rejuvenated. At eighty, he has the physical stamina of his younger crew members but the wisdom of a man old enough to be the father of the most mature among them.

The inevitable sociopolitical implications of SF are exemplified here by Bradbury's futuristic novel making it possible for his American science to recover and preserve what American society has often until now held in contempt: the wisdom of the elderly. American society is regarded with horror by other cultures for the way it considers the sagacity and experience of great-grandparents as irrelevant, superflous, comical. Bradbury's creation of Captain Black restores dignity to the American octogenarian.

Closer to science fantasy is Bradbury's T-S-H (see "The Earth Men" discussion), which is greatly developed and refined in this tale. Telepathic powers resided only in the woman in "Ylla;" then in some women, children, and artists in "The Summer Night;" but also in psychotics in "The Earth Men," In "The Third Expedition," apparently, The Martians in charge have seen to it that only telepaths are allowed to be in the company of the Earth Men. And these selected telepaths apparently include only those with hypnotic and projective powers, such as we first met in "The Earth Men," except that here these are not psychotics.

Once we reach the last page, and reflect back on the other stories, we can put all the clues together to understand Bradbury's most elaborate version yet of the several elements of his T-S-H. Through telepathy, some Martians can read the minds of the crewmen in the spaceship, especially ransacking their memories of relatives and family history. Partly through hypnosis, these Martians can delude the crew into seeing Martians as their own dead relatives brought back to life, the Martian buildings as Earth dwellings, and the planet Mars as a happy heaven for Earth's "dear departed." Partly, too, this is achieved through the Martians' talent in projection of their own ideas, images that they can will into three-dimensionality by their advanced holography. And, of course, the crewmen cooperate by seeing, hearing, and feeling what they want to.

Combining these several factors makes it possible for Bradbury to build up to a crucial dramatic moment. A Martian, seen by the crew as Lustig's grandmother, tells the captain, who thinks his men are seeing ghosts, to feel her wrist. "Solid, ain't it?"

A MAJOR SF CHARACTERISTIC
Granted. "The Third," with its emotional appeal grounded in our awe and fear of death and its aftermath, is a true horror story. But we must also concede that the story gains much of its suspense and its resolution from a major characteristic of SF. What is continuously operating here is the tireless, dedicated scientific curiosity of the characters. This feature of SF makes it a medium for the enjoyment of logical discussion, the endless pursuit of ideas, and hypothesizing and rehypothesizing.

Classical precedents can be found in Verne and Wells. In Verne's *Twenty Thousand Leagues Under the Sea*, the characters discuss rival theories of atoll formation, the illusion and reality of giant squid, the possibilities of towns of people living under water. In Wells's *War of the Worlds*, the narrator explains the kind of technology possible without the wheel, and how extraterrestrial life is most likely to succumb to bacteria never encountered before their arrival on Earth. SF is a sunny realm for those who relish both imagination and intellectual exercise in their reading.

In "The Third," such rational probing begins with the crew's various hypotheses about the Martian scene outside the ship. Have they unwittingly traveled back through time, on Earth itself, instead of traveling to Mars? Are they trapped in the past? Is this midwestern town the work of York and Williams? A dozen such questions make for a kind of massive suspense. And it's such persistent inquiry that finally makes it possible for Captain Black to understand their predicament. This brings us to a true catharsis. Even though the ending is tragic, it does bring complete insight into what was a total mystery.

"HORROR IN DISGUISE"

The ghostly quality of "The Third" must figure in any effort to classify it by genre. Jack Sullivan, in his authoritative *Penguin Encyclopedia of Horror*, notes that some of Bradbury's SF is really "horror in disguise." Our present story, he says, "is a ghost story, and a thoroughly malevolent one at that."

SETTING

Such stories, Sullivan continues, "reveal the dark side of Bradbury's nostalgia." Sullivan is referring to the fact, often explored by the critics, that even when Bradbury's fiction is set on Mars, his real setting is "a dreamlike little town, a memory projected onto another planet." The dream town of course is always Waukegan, Illinois (see Chapter 1). In "The Third," Waukegan is called Green Bluff, Illinois. In other stories, it is called Green Town, Illinois.

CHARACTERIZATION

It is his power to drive through to insight that makes Captain Black the captain. And Bradbury is emphatic about it; it is Black's age, his eighty years' experience and cumulative wisdom, that makes him the best thinker in the crew. Through Black, wisdom is characterized as the ability to postpone conclusions and to reopen the question, again and again. No other American character is—or need be—so thoroughly developed as Black. Among the Martians, it is John Black's "brother Edward" who is the most fully portrayed. He has been entrusted by his people with the most difficult mission of all—to keep the Captain, the strongest intellect in the crew, deceived until he falls asleep and can be disposed of. Note that Edward is tested twice. When the captain asks about their sister Marilyn, "Edward" must pause. Apparently there were some gaps in their mind-reading. And then the captain reconstructs the entire truth and "Edward" must act fast before his "brother" can alert his other fifteen crewmen.

MOTIVATION: TELEVISION VERSION

If you can locate a video of the television play, note that here Matheson achieved one of his few improvements on the original story. He has Edward telling John (dying of poison) why the Martians had to do this: The Americans came armed with nuclear weapons.

THEMES

Bradbury's message is clear. Human survival depends on the most persistent use of experience and intelligence, so much so that we must keep our elders in good health so we can use their higher wisdom. Even so, humanity's nemesis could be extraterrestrials with a different kind of intelligence (and more than five senses?), "incredibly brilliant," as Black thinks the Martians are.

POINT OF VIEW

Bradbury uses the authorial voice here much as he did in "The Earth Men." He tells the story in the author's voice but from the point of view of the Americans, until they are destroyed, and then he narrates the ending from the point of view of the author omniscient.

NOVEL STRUCTURE

So far, three expeditions have failed to establish a foothold on Mars. With the next story, however, successful settlement of the planet begins. Some critics (e.g., Wayne Johnson) see at this point a dividing line between an introductory section, or a prologue and the main body of the novel, consisting of the next thirteen chronicles. (See "Plot: Mythic Structure, Plus," Chapter 4, and "Structural Function" in our discussion of "The Luggage Store" later in this chapter.)

JUNE 2001:—AND THE MOON BE STILL AS BRIGHT

TITLE AND SETTING

The name of the poem from which Bradbury takes his title is "So, We'll Go No More A Roving," written by George Gordon, Lord Byron, in 1817. Spender's recitation gives us one of the most poetic/dramatic moments in all SF: double-shadow moonlight on a strange planet, a party of newly arrived United States space men walking through a "dreaming dead city," whispering in involuntary awe, pausing on a tiled avenue, hearing their archaeologist explain that this poem could have been written by the last Martian poet.

Byron's twelve-line, three-stanza ballad-lyric expresses the passionate awareness that someday life itself must slow down, "love itself must rest," even though Nature itself (as symbolized by the moon) seems eternal. The tragedy of the decline of Martian culture, which causes archaeologist Spender's grieving need to recite Byron, of course affects the rest of the crew— even if subliminally—because it reminds them of their own and their civilization's mortality.

THEMES: TECHNIQUE

This story offers us one of the fullest statements of Bradbury's sociopolitical views to be found anywhere in his vast oeuvre.

Usually, Bradbury, like any writer of artistic fiction, implies his views mainly through the results of his action, conflicts, and character development; occasionally, as we've seen in "The Taxpayer," he delivers his opinions through the speech of a "chorus character."

In "—And the Moon Be Still as Bright" he makes full use of all these techniques but with extraordinary emphasis on explicit philosophizing by Spender, the disaffected American. Such quasimoralizing is risky. Bradbury carries it off easily, makes us enjoy Spender's intelligent griping by building up terrific suspense, by making us see the need for one of the most intellectual parleys ever held during mortal combat. In other words the artistic problem was to motivate both characters and readers to accept—nay, to need—a philosophical disquisition on America's worst faults. Bradbury does it here for the Americans as well as G. B. Shaw does it for Englishmen. To compare Bradbury's success with a near failure of this kind of effort, contrast his philosophizing in *Chronicles* with Edward Bellamy's in *Looking Backward*.

Incidentally, if you're new to SF, you should know that SF aficionados are open indeed to the severest criticism of their own society.

THEMES: MESSAGE
Bradbury's thematic materials in this story may be grouped under two headings, the first relatively unusual, the second one of his chronic themes: 1) All-out challenge to American values; 2) Metamorphosis, here manifest in a) changes, good and bad, brought about in a mythic utopian Mars by internal and external pressures, and b) changes in character among American explorers of that culture.

CHALLENGE TO UNITED STATES VALUES
Mainly through Spender; and to a lesser extent, through a Spender convert, Captain Wilder; and through a symbolic event, Bradbury delivers an all-out assault on American beliefs and behavior, specifically on:

1. Americans' disrespect for anything different from their own lives, their values, themselves.

2. The tyranny of American "commercial . . . [and] power interests" over human and cultural considerations.

3. The artificial dichotomies in American culture between life and art, between science and religion, between the mental and the animal life, between technology and Nature (including contempt for the environment).

4. The tyranny of the majority, which is often blind, bumbling, misinformed, easily misled.

5. Americans' disproportionate acceptance of Darwin (to the detriment of religion, or a belief in purpose) and of Freud (to the detriment of respect for the creative artist). This criticism is vaguely stated and not as well-developed as the others, so do not blame yourself if you do not "get" it.

6. Americans' blind development of technology without parallel development of ethics and social consciousness.

Generally, Americans are compared with Cortez and his followers: "greedy, righteous bigots" who believe "catch as catch can, finder's keepers, if the other fellow turns his cheek, slap it hard . . ."

METAMORPHOSES IN MARS
It serves Bradbury's purpose—in using Mars as a contrast to the United States—to represent the "Red Planet" as having gone through three major changes in its long history: 1) Martians developed an advanced technology "as good as anything we'll ever hope to have." 2) But they stopped progress at that point where science threatened to crush religion, ethics, and esthetics. In slowing technological progress they ended wars and began to enjoy life for the sheer pleasure of living it. Spender says the Martians "stopped where we should have

stopped a hundred years ago." Since this story is set in 2001, Spender means Earth should have declared a moratorium on scientific advance about 1901. 3) But, as the crew's physician-geologist Hathaway has discovered, most Martians have recently been wiped out by smallpox, i.e., by disease brought from Earth that Martians had never encountered and so had no defenses against.

SF THEME OF INTERPLANETARY CONTAGION

> In 1952, I met, in the jungles of southern Mexico, a Danish anthropologist in a state of shock. He had visited a secluded Indian tribe that had never been exposed to the white man's cold viruses. He himself had a mild cold which the Indians caught: it wiped out two-thirds of the tribe in a fortnight.

Such involuntary intercultural germ-warfare was so well known to science that as early as 1895, when he was working on his novel *The War of the Worlds*, H. G. Wells used a version of it to end the invasion of Earth by Martians. The Red Planeteers die of terrestrial bacteria they were unprepared to fight. Interplanetary contamination became a stock theme in SF. By the same token, American astronauts actually were carefully examined and quarantined when they returned from the moon to make sure they had not brought back to Earth any strain of virus Earth could not withstand.

SYMBOLIC EVENT

Extermination of the Martians, by Earth men's introduction of a child's disease not fatal on Earth, becomes symbolic of the careless damage that interplanetary exploration can cause to other civilizations. This is one of the reasons Spender wants Earth's archaeologists to have fifty years alone on Mars before untrained laymen are admitted there.

METAMORPHOSES IN CHARACTER: SPENDER

The first archaeologist on Mars is one of Bradbury's most complex characters. From the beginning he is represented as a loner, an outsider. He doesn't want to use a manmade stove to keep himself warm on Mars: it would an "imported blasphemy." Instead he uses Martian wood to build a fire on Mars. He is opposed to a "celebration" on their first night in a place where a civilization is dying. He is obviously accepted by the others as abnormal but it's equally obvious he's never done anything so antisocial as to disqualify him from his profession and the expedition. And now suddenly his behavior becomes first pugnacious and then murderous.

Bradbury motivates this extreme change convincingly. Actually, it began on Earth when Congress announced plans to set up nuclear arsenals on Mars. Instead of using Martian expeditions to learn about and from another way of life, Spender's country is ready simply to impose its present colonizing ways on an innocent civilization. Spender is desperate to prevent this, if possible to hold off colonization and destruction of a beautiful civilization until science can preserve its beauty and its advanced values. He knows he cannot convince the crew to see this point of view and he considers this a situation where the majority is wrong. Bradbury sees to it that, faced with a choice between Biggs's vulgar values and Spender's enlightened views, we would rather give the latter a chance. But we recoil at what Spender sees as the logical next step: he must become a Martian and defend Mars against Earth men by treating them as invaders.

Bradbury is careful to see that not all Spender's conflicts are with external forces. Spender suffers internal conflicts at several points, now determined to wipe out the invaders, now sickened by the slaughter he has triggered, now resolved again to carry out his plan to its logical conclusion.

CHEROKEE'S METAMORPHOSIS

Bradbury's excellent characterization of Spender is achieved partly through comparing the archaeologist with two crewmen: Cherokee and Captain Wilder. An Indian by blood, Cherokee doesn't want to see the Martians treated by the United States as were the Cherokee. But he also cannot condone Spender's treatment of the white man: summary execution. Cherokee has a chance to live by joining Spender, but instead dies for his own humane values.

WILDER'S METAMORPHOSIS

Like Captain Black, Captain Wilder deserves his rank because of his far superior intelligence and his Montaignean tolerance for other points of view (see our discussion of "The Earth Men"). In his impartiality, Wilder can see the value of Biggs's efforts to make the crew "get happy." Wilder is curious and respectful of Spender's aims on Mars, and he uses every minute before he has to kill Spender to learn from him. We soon see why. He feels he has to become the new Spender: a man with Spender's values but without, he hopes, Spender's extreme methods. Wilder has learned from Spender to distrust the "rotten majority." At the end, when Wilder punishes Parkhill for desecrating Martian architecture, we have the uneasy sense that Wilder will find it hard to adopt only Spender's values without his wrath.

SYMBOLISM: THE FATAL WOUND

Bradbury finds a compelling way to symbolize Wilder's respect for Spender. The Captain's refusal to use grenades, his insistence that his men aim only at Spender's chest (his intention, in other words to keep Spender's head intact) are emblematic of his desire to maintain the integrity of his ideas. Notice that Spender himself understands what Wilder is doing. Realizing that without Cherokee and Wilder he has no hope, Spender offers Wilder the perfect target he wants: Spender's chest exposed in a cleft in the rocks accessible only to Wilder's line of sight. Wilder's burying Spender in a Martian sarcophagus is Wilder's way of respecting Spender as a Martian.

SETTING

In his *Ray Bradbury and the Poetics of Reverie*, W. F. Touponce says *Chronicles* "bears no resemblance to the known scientific facts about Mars, except that it is the next planet out from the sun after Earth." But the setting of our present story does include three additional resemblances to the known facts: Bradbury's Mars has two moons, dust storms, deserts.

SETTING: LOWELLIAN INFLUENCE

Bradbury's setting also includes the canals that Lowell thought he saw on Mars: the canals on which he based his argument that an advanced civilization existed on the Red Planet (see Chapter 2). It is important to note that 1) *Chronicles* was published in 1950 and that 2) in their *Life Beyond Earth*, scientists Gerald Feinberg and Robert Shapiro recall that as late as "the early 1960s . . . canals were not fully eliminated from consideration." Today these phenomena are more properly called *channels*. Great in number in the older terrain of Mars' southern hemisphere, they are tens of miles wide and hundreds of miles long.

CLASSICAL PARALLELS

The aesthetic and philosophical values Spender finds in the Martian civilization are definitely classical Greek, especially the emphasis on balance, harmony, and serenity. Wayne Johnson, in his *Ray Bradbury*, sees the friezes of beautiful animals, men and women, and sun symbols as suggesting "the Martians practiced a sort of Greek pantheism," that is, a religion in which divinity is inherent in all reality. The marble fixtures in these friezes, however, seem more Minoan or Egyptian than Greek. Obviously, Bradbury combines suggestion, once again, with the specific.

PARALLEL WITH COLLIER

Spender's ideas are quite parallel to those of John Collier (1884–1968), President Franklin Roosevelt's Commissioner of American Indian Affairs. In his book *The Long Hope*—published in 1947, when Bradbury was working on *Chronicles*—Collier explains the need for the white man to learn what the Indian has to teach: how to survive in harmony with inner and outer Nature, for instance. This is similar to Spender's insistence that the Americans learn from Martian civilization before they overrun it. (*The Long Hope* is retitled *Indians of the Americas* in its paperback editions.)

STYLE: CITY METAPHOR

Bradbury uses a striking simile to describe a Martian city sky-line, which looks like sharply carved chess pieces. This suggests an architecture of greatly varied shapes (more Mexican than norteamericano). In "Ylla" Bradbury used the same image in a more compact (and mysterious) metaphor: bone-chess cities.

STYLE: SENSUOUS DETAIL

Descriptions are achieved with Bradbury's usual rich appeal to our senses. Biggs's body drifts with slow unconcern, making a hollow bubbling sound. After Wilder shoots, the rocks changed color under Spender.

POINT OF VIEW

Bradbury tells his story in his own authorial voice but limits himself now to Spender's point of now, now to Wilder's. Many of the shifts are the narrative equivalent of the cinematic "reverse POV" shots.

AUGUST 2001: THE SETTLERS

This interchapter is characterized by insistent parallel structure as Bradbury focuses on two psychological aspects of the settlements: the reasons men migrate (as many reasons as men), and their initial loneliness. The climax of this little prose poem consists of an imaginative view of their native land as they see it shrinking beneath, then behind them. The structural function is twofold: to return us briefly to the general overall situation before we experience another, fuller account of specific explorers; and to prepare us for the mood, the loneliness, the unique purpose of one of these special pioneers.

DECEMBER 2001: THE GREEN MORNING

POINT OF VIEW

In his interchapter "The Settlers," Bradbury pulled back to become the author omniscient, capable of a godlike overview of space and time. Now he zooms in again for his favorite narrative stance—that of the author limited to the point of view of just one character.

HISTORICAL BACKGROUND AND PARALLELS

Bradbury models this short story on the life of the legendary frontiersman, "Johnny Appleseed," born John Chapman in Massachusetts in 1774. At age twenty-six, he appeared in Pennsylvania to begin his forty-year self-appointed task of planting apple seeds along roads and trails clear across Ohio and Indiana. He devoted himself generally to the public good, for example, warning frontier settlers of the movements of hostile Indian tribes. Like Chapman, Bradbury's Benjamin Driscoll is also a pioneer, and he too has volunteered to plant trees (on treeless Mars). Like Chapman, as portrayed in statues of him outside Johnny Appleseed restaurants, Driscoll is slight of physique. But Chapman, as Driscoll sees his role model, had a relatively limited goal: to provide fruit for future generations, while Driscoll hopes to grow all species of trees to provide a more basic and general human need: more oxygen in Mars' atmosphere.

SF AND SCIENTIFIC BACKGROUND

Plant life absorbs carbon dioxide from the atmosphere and gives off oxygen. Although this exchange is not mentioned in the story, it is interesting to note that in 1948, just two years before Bradbury published *Chronicles*, the astronomer Gerard Peter Kuiper demonstrated that the atmosphere of Mars is ninety-five percent carbon dioxide.

The hydroponic plants Bradbury says some settlers are growing are cultivated not in soil but in water that contains dissolved nutrients. This garden-scale effort provides a timid contrast to Driscoll's bold project. A Bradbury conception that will come true is Driscoll's use of a pack made of transparent plastic: every item can be located easily. A poetic bit of SF is Bradbury's conceit of frosted-food ships as flying icicles.

STORY STRUCTURE
The story unfolds in continuous action over two days with the general background situation and events of the past thirty days recalled as flashbacks in Driscoll's brooding over his hopes. Note that Bradbury marks both the low point and the high point of Driscoll's experience with fainting spells: the first for lack of oxygen, the second from the sudden change in atmosphere as well as from Driscoll's excitement over his fantastic success.

MOTIVATION
Bradbury conceives of both unique personal and general social reasons for Driscoll's inspiration. Driscoll is quite determined to stay on Mars. And so when a physician threatens to return him to Earth because of his fainting in the thin air, Driscoll thinks rather of enriching the air! Also, Spender's prediction has become a truth that figures in Driscoll's motivation. All the other settlers are too busy ransacking Mars for its mineral wealth to think of planting arboretums.

SENSUOUS DETAIL AND METAPHOR
Bradbury's talent with images makes the action colorful and dramatic. When Driscoll struggles for oxygen, Bradbury pictures him like another creature out of his element, gasping in horrid fishlike motions. When rain pelts his fire, Driscoll thinks it looks as if an invisible animal is dancing on it and the rain has a peppery taste. And even the story's title is a metaphor.

PART 3

FEBRUARY 2002: THE LOCUSTS

TITLE AND METAPHOR
Locusts are migratory grasshoppers that, under certain conditions, take to the air in swarms of billions. When they settle down, they destroy the agriculture. These insects provide the

perfect metaphor for Bradbury's rockets, which are swarming to Mars and destroying its landscape . . . and its culture.

POINT OF VIEW AND STRUCTURAL FUNCTION
Bradbury pulls back from his closeup of Driscoll in "The Green Morning" to take another overview of the general expeditionary situation, writing briefly as author omniscient (before zooming in again to study a specific situation on Mars from the point of view of one character in "Night Meeting").

THEMES
Into this brief, fiercely written interlude, Bradbury crowds grim illustrations of three themes: 1) Spender's charge that Americans disrespect anything different from themselves and their own creations. As quickly as possible, the settlers want Mars to be America. They lack the curiosity and patience to discover the indigenous Mars and to blend its features and values into their own. 2) American fear of silence. Other American writers who have discussed this characteristic are Joseph Wood Krutch, in his essay "Back to God's Concrete," and William Faulkner in his novel *Intruder in the Dust.* They agree that Americans need continuous sounds because *silence can lead to thinking which may prove to be open-ended. . . .* 3) Metamorphosis. And so, quiet and strangely different Mars is transformed into a noisy, familiar American settlement.

MASTER IMAGE
The main literary feature of this vigorous prose poem is the unforgettable image of the frenetic carpenters with their mouths fringed with nails so they resembled steel-toothed carnivores, spitting them into their hands rapid-fire and hammering them into the frames for cottages.

AUGUST 2002: NIGHT MEETING

A CONVERSATION PIECE
"Night Meeting" is a story that is eminently open to discussion. Even readers who rarely try to "critique" fiction will find themselves talking in some wonderment about this fantasy-piece:

about the beautiful peaceful quality of the chance encounter of two ordinary citizens from two different planets; about the manic monologue of the lovable old gas-station owner; about Bradbury's mysterious adventures here with the nature of Time.

MUSICAL STRUCTURE

Note first the way "Night Meeting" is structured internally and the way it relates externally to earlier pieces. It is divided into three situations: Tomas Gomez's talk, at the out-of-the-way gas station, with Pop the owner; Tomas's long lonely drive; and his meeting with Martian Muhe Ca. But Pop's long answers to Tomas's short questions also relate in part to "The Locusts" and "The Green Morning," giving us a sharp contrast to the attitude of the steel-toothed settlers and the miners in those preceding chronicles. And Pop's monologue is not only a tie-back to earlier pieces, it is also a foreshadowing of the Gomez-Ca encounter. This thematic echoing back and hinting ahead is the kind of structure that George Edgar Slusser must have had in mind when he wrote that *Chronicles* is Bradbury's

> . . . masterpiece of lyrical organization; its themes, tones, and variations in length and mood are woven into a subtle pattern of resonances—counterpoint and contrast that are musical in nature.

Unfortunately, Slusser rarely develops such insights as they deserve to be developed, preferring perhaps to let others follow through as we are doing here.

CHARACTERIZATION:
THE DANIEL BOONE MENTALITY

"The Locusts" characterizes the typical settlers as eager to suppress the differences between Martian and United States culture, and to impose instead familiar American qualities on Mars. Pop, however, is a nonconformist. He enjoys the differences between Earth and Mars. Indeed, if the American settlements encroach too much on his station, he will move it further out into the wilderness. This is a Daniel Boone characteristic, a subtle aspect of that pioneer not often stressed in the simplistic legends about him. Boone always moved further west when settlers brought their noisy crossroads towns into his quiet wilderness; his preferences were often for the Indian, not the Anglo life-style; and he retired not to the work-ethic culture of the American but to the more relaxed style of the Spanish settler.

Pop thus becomes one of Bradbury's outsiders, allied in varying degrees with archaeologist Spender, tree-planter Driscoll, and Fireman Montag (*Fahrenheit 451*). And when Tomas drives off for a long communion with quiet Nature, he proves to be a less garrulous practitioner of similar minority views.

FORESHADOWING

Pop admits he's never seen a Martian, but he hears they're around and "crazy," and obviously their craziness does not repel but rather intrigues him. Then, a crucial point for our understanding the theme: Pop says even Time is crazy on Mars! Then Tomas's feelings continue the foreshadowing as he explores mentally the sound, smell, and texture of Time, a brilliant but typical Bradbury excursion. These three hints prepare us not only for Tomas's first sight of a live Martian but also for the meaning of their "ghostly" experience with each other.

CHARACTERIZATION: THE OPEN MIND

Just imagine what American Biggs or Parkhill would do to Muhe Ca, or what Martian Xxx would do to Gomez! Then we realize what it is that Bradbury is saying here: When Earth people and extraterrestrials do meet, let them be persons with open minds, curiosity, no ax to grind, "laid back" people excited by differences as well as by similarities. Both are important: Gomez and Ca reach each other because they are sufficiently similar in their curiosity, openmindedness, and pacifism to appreciate the ways they are different.

NATURE OF TIME

Early in 1987 the explosion of a supernova was first sighted by Earth people. From then on, astronomers could observe a major happening that wasn't happening. For, of course, the real explosion had occurred millions of years ago and the light rays from it are just now reaching Earth. But, of course, it's also true that this major happening was happening—here. The time-space continuum, by its very nature, structures—as it does in the supernova observation—a simultaneity of the distant past and the now.

I see this as the scientific background for understanding the "ghostly" meeting between Ca and Gomez. The Martian and the American are living in two different time sequences. They have met in some tunnel of beyond-the-third (fourth? tenth?) dimension where all Time can be seen as simultaneous by those able to see that way at all. Apparently, they both entered such a tunnel when they both coincidentally felt, a ways back before their paths converged, certain changes in the light and temperature. They can only partly experience each other just as we can only partly experience the supernova. Bradbury choose sight and mind-reading as two of the ways they can communicate, and touch as one of the ways they cannot relate.

MINDSET IN COMMUNICATION
It is possible that Bradbury is also saying that Ca and Gomez are accessible to each other only because they have the mental capacity for multicultural sensitivity; that Parkhill and Ca would never "meet," Biggs just never see Ca.

SEEING OTHER STRANGE THINGS
Just as Gomez's open mindset makes it possible for him to see Ca, so it makes it possible for him to realize that the Martians can ride vehicles that move not on wheels but on legs just as a praying mantis moves on its six limbs. Here Bradbury explores the possibilities of non-wheel motivity that H. G. Wells also explored in *The War of the Worlds*. But just as Tomas and Muhe cannot touch, so even their extraordinary vision has its limitations: neither can see the other's world-at-large, a world alternative to their own, both staged simultaneously on the same terrain.

THEMES

"Night Meeting," then, is informed by old and new Bradbury themes. Old, that one's point of view and orientation affect one's perception of reality. New, that so far as possible, inter-planetary exploration, being potentially psychological as well as definitely physical in nature, must be entrusted to men like Pop and Gomez; that these people need not be so sophisti-cated as Spender, Black, or Wilder. Just naive, in the best sense of the word: open-minded, uncorrupted.

SHIFT IN POINT OF VIEW

From Gomez's meeting with Pop to that with Ca, Bradbury perceived all the action from Gomez's point of view . . . until, very near the end, Bradbury becomes the author omniscient, able to shift us suddenly inside Ca's thoughts as well. This brief shift makes it possible for us to compare the American's and the Martian's views. It also fits in well with Bradbury's penchant for broadening the point of view at the end of the story. (Compare this shift in "Night Meeting" with that in "The Earth Men" and "The Third Expedition.")

AUTOBIOGRAPHICAL ELEMENTS

One of Bradbury's two openminded Americans is Hispanic in origin. Bradbury spent many years living in a Chicano slum in California. If you are interested in his fictitious use of his experiences with Spanish-speaking Americans, start with *Death is a Lonely Business* (1985).

OCTOBER 2002: THE SHORE

STRUCTURAL FUNCTION

Up to this point Bradbury has given us six stories, five of them preceded by interchapters, sketches, vignettes, or interludes, as we have variously called them (Johnson calls them bridges). Now, Bradbury breaks the rhythm and gives us three such short sketches in succession. The purpose of most of the inter-chapters remains the same: usually to zoom back and give us a broad, general overview of the expeditions before we zoom in again for a close look at the fortunes of one special group with developed characters.

TITLE
"The Shore" is Bradbury's metaphor for Mars because it attracts waves of men coming in over the sea of space.

TYPOLOGY AND HISTORY
Bradbury attempts some rough classification of the kinds of people who make up the waves. Apparently, he has modeled them, and the order of their migration, upon the historical settlement of the American West, Australia, and Alaska. He sees the first wave as tough outdoorsmen, loners, typical pioneers; the "second men" as, apparently, from the lower classes, urban and rural, migrating for economic reasons. The "seconds" include a few who are either mystics, wildeyed idealists, or men terminally ill: It's hard to say from Bradbury's cryptic description of them as looking "as if they were on their way to God."

SOUR NOTES AND A PROPHECY
Bradbury hints, rather sarcastically, who the "first women" are by saying that "Everyone knew who they would be." If the analogy is being made to the Old West, these are the prostitutes who follow all-male migrations, like prospecting expeditions, fur-trapping, companies, military campaigns. Bradbury's mention of them is tinged with contempt and no sympathy; there is no recognition that they are, as much as Ylla, victims of a man's world.

In his authorial voice, Bradbury offers the opinion that there should have been men from other countries to guarantee a healthy diversity of ideas, but since the United States owns the rockets, it keeps the glory and its profits to itself. Bradbury is prophetic here. Almost forty years after he wrote this passage, the *New York Times* would report that "American officials . . . are downplaying international cooperation as a factor" in United States plans to place a man on Mars; " . . . the main objective is to assert American leadership in space."

Bradbury omits any mention here of who the "second women" are. By analogy again, they would be those valiant women who accompany the settlers who follow the pioneers. But Bradbury compensates for this omission elsewhere: there are women back in "The Locusts" and ahead in "The Musicians."

FEBRUARY 2003: INTERIM

This sketch offers a variation on one of Bradbury's main themes: Americans are so uninterested in the new possibilities in a strange place that they hasten to replicate, in detail, their own earlier way of life. He compares Tenth City with an Iowa town lifted by a twister and dropped beside a Mars canal. (See "Structural Function" in our discussion of "The Shore.")

APRIL 2003: THE MUSICIANS

METAPHOR AND METAMORPHOSIS

This ingenious but macabre interchapter is rich in metaphor and allusions to other Bradbury stories. The theme is metamorphosis as illustrated in the decaying corpses of Martians and in the daring pranks of American boys in their first—and forbidden—brush with death. A basic simile in this sketch first appeared in "—And the Moon Be Still as Bright," when Hathaway reported that passing through rooms of dead Martians was like walking in a pile of autumn leaves. The boys are warned not to visit these rooms; their disobedience is discovered whenever their mothers find "black flakelets" on their shoes. Other macabre metaphors: The bones of the dead are *peppermint sticks* or *xylophone bones*, and boys bold enough to play on them are the musicians of the title. It is a tribute to Bradbury's literary intensity that such a short piece can communicate so vividly the quality of the child's passage from ignorance-and-innocence to knowledge-and-independence.

BRADBURY'S FIREMEN

Another allusion consists in the reason for the boys' haste in visiting as many of the dead as possible: The sanitary Firemen will soon come to burn the "autumn leaves" and "xylophones." Firemen usually put fires out, not start them. But in 1950—the same year that *Chronicles* appeared—Bradbury published in *Galaxy* a story titled "The Fireman," about public officials who burn books and so sanitize the community. That story was later expanded into the 1953 novel, *Fahrenheit 451*. The brief mention of the Firemen here in "The Musicians" serves too as foreshadowing of "Usher II," one of the *Chronicles* for 2005.

STRUCTURAL FUNCTION

We have classified "The Musicians" as one of the "overview interchapters" because it generalizes about settlers' behavior more than it details specific actions by individual characters who are developed. The point of view, as in all the interchapters, is that of the author omniscient.

JUNE 2003: WAY IN THE MIDDLE OF THE AIR

THEMES: SPECULATIVE FICTION

During the period of undisguised slavery in the United States, some blacks were able to escape to Canada with the help of an interracial network called the Underground Railway. In this story, Bradbury updates the concept. He builds his plot—as all speculative fiction is built—on a series of IFs:

1. IF travel to Mars is feasible, and IF one of the reasons people emigrate is to leave persecution and discrimination behind, surely black Americans would be among the first to escape to the "Red Planet."

2. IF such a great technical feat could be achieved, how would the emigres handle such problems as the debts some blacks owe to whites? As one of Bradbury's white characters is astonished to see, "Them that has helps them that hasn't." This leaves white America with a grave sociopsychological question, as follows.

3. IF the blacks all escape Earth, what would the racist mentality do when it is left with nobody to scorn, bully, exploit, torture, and lynch? (This story was published in 1950 when all such racist activities were common in the

United States and when it was highly uncommon for white authors to write antiracist stories.)

SETTING

Bradbury's setting suggests that he visualized the action being produced on a stage with a single set. With many different characters making a series of appearances before that single set, the story takes on the ambience of a classical Greek drama. Eight of the nine successive situations that make up the story occur on or in front of the porch of an old-fashioned hardware store, presumably on the road the blacks must take to board the rockets. The eighth of the nine story segments—the futile automobile chase—does take place out on that road, but if the story were presented on stage (as we suggest you try in "Ideas for Papers and Oral Reports") that segment could simply be recounted by the two men who attempt the pursuit when they return. This setting is ideal for several reasons. It is central to the action; it provides unity and continuity; it is symbolic, for this is where the racists buy the rope, the guns, the ammunition with which they terrorize all—and kill some—of the black folk.

MASTER METAPHOR

Bradbury uses the levee that holds back the flood—a common sight in many southern towns—as a master metaphor. The levee stands for white control of the black populace; and when it breaks, the resulting flood is a black river tearing its way between the white banks of the town, free and irresistible.

SIMILES

Our highly imaginative author sees watermelons lying in the meadows as *striped like turquoise cats*; the white men sitting on the porch *like nervous hounds*; the white women, come to plead with their husbands to stop this exodus of the servant class, *rustling like ancient papers*; the racists in a car—with their knees and guns sticking up sharp—resembling a *carload of cranes*.

CONFLICTS AND CHARACTERIZATION

The basic conflict is between the blacks, escaping in a steady stream, and the whites, caught by surprise, hoping but unable to stem the tide. We do not expect any character development in the leader of the whites, the hardware owner; Bradbury's punch line makes it clear that Mr. Teece will always need to feel superior to someone. And from the way he treats his wife, we may guess that in their sick need of scapegoats, the white men will hereafter act even more harshly toward their women and children.

But Bradbury does make the other men on the porch capable of internal conflict, hence of growth. The story enters its long crisis when white Grandpa offers to do the menial work that Teece insists the black boy Silly stay behind to do. Grandpa's defiance of Teece encourages other whites to insist that Teece accept the situation. Their courage seems all the greater when we recall that Teece pointed out, earlier, that he's good at shooting whites too.

The most courageous person, though, probably one of the sweetest boys in all contemporary literature, is Silly—and one of the smartest, we might add. Thanks to the concerted effort of his people, he develops from a servile errand boy into a person with dignity and a future. It is satisfying that Bradbury gives to Silly the line that throws Teece off balance and exposes him to us as a chronic lyncher: "What you goin' to do nights, Mr. Teece?"

POINT OF VIEW

Here, Bradbury uses a point of view unusual in this book. So far, he has written as the author omniscient in the interchapters, and as author as limited narrator in the full-length stories. In this latter stance he has always limited himself to the point of view of one character (at a time) and has always taken us inside that character. In "Way in the Middle of the Sky," however, he uses a third point of view. He is inside no character, viewing the action from outside all characters. We could call this Bradbury's author as *objective narrator* point of view. He uses it once again in "The Off Season." See the section "Character Self-evaluation" in Chapter 4, for more details about the effects of this point of view.

PART 4

2004–05: THE NAMING OF NAMES

THE TITLE
Like many Bradbury phrases, "The Naming of Names" resonates with multiple meanings. On the level of sheer love of language, it is a repetition in which the process and its result are celebrated side-by-side, as in "the singing of songs" or "the painting of paintings." On another level, it expands on a conversation Spender the archaeologist had with Captain Wilder ("—And the Moon Be Still as Bright"). Spender saw the mountains, hills, and canals as sacredly forever Martian. He dreaded the way Americans would violate that sacredness by imposing their own new and irrelevant names on places that already bore ancient, meaningful, Martian titles. Captain Wilder replied that it was the archaeologist's job to discover those Martian names and then "we'll use them." Apparently Bradbury now wants us to understand that Wilder promised more than he could deliver, and Spender's prediction was borne out. Although this interlude implies that the Martian names are now (2005) known, in its list of place names it gives only familiar American proper nouns. Ironically, the two idealists are memorialized in Wilder Town and Spender Hill. On still another level, "the naming of names" can refer to abstract intellectual processes, e.g., as performed by sociologists formulating "laws." Bradbury's point then would be that these "sophisticates" are dealing not with specific and concrete things but with words related to other words, gearing generalization to generalization.

STRUCTURAL FUNCTION
After Bradbury has dealt in detail with one group of characters in a small locale ("Way in the Middle of the Sky"), he zooms

back again to get—in this interchapter—a general overview of the migrations and to provide background for the next story. His last sentence here indicates he is ready to zoom in again for a detailed narration of some other local situation. The point of view, as in all the interchapters, is that of the author omniscient.

THEME: METAMORPHOSIS, DIALETIC

In this one-page over-view Bradbury gives us what amounts to a theory of history. The migrations are changing in nature so fast that now it's not just random metamorphosis, it is a Hegelian dialectic. The expeditions were launched by pioneers, explorers of frontiers—they were heroic, adventurous. Since the settlements are now secure, "sophisticates" are moving in, exploiting advantages created by their forerunners, bringing with them regularity, organization, abstract pursuits, bureaucracy. And so the Hegelian dialectic is set in motion, as those who don't like being so controlled strike back.

AUTOBIOGRAPHICAL BACKGROUND

Such striking back is based in part on Bradbury's own experiences early in life. Just as on Mars now (2005) there are those who "plan people's lives and libraries," so in his youth there were people who criticized his love of circuses and comics as "vulgar." Intimidated, he tore up his collection of Buck Rogers comic strips. For a month he felt desolate. Then he "pushed back," resuming his affair with SF comics, defying "friends" who had tried to plan his life and library. "My life has been happy ever since," he recalls in "Drunk, and in Charge of a Bicycle," his introduction to his 885-page volume, *The Stories of Ray Bradbury* (1980).

APRIL 2005: USHER II

IMPORTANCE

This story ranks high in contemporary literature on several grounds: as political satire, as black humor, as a dystopian work, as a horror story, as science fantasy, as a literary tour de force.

TITLE

"Usher II" promises us some kind of sequel to Edgar Allan Poe's "The Fall of the House of Usher." The more that readers know of Poe's fiction, the more facets of Bradbury's tale they can enjoy. But readers unfamiliar with Poe will still find that Bradbury supplies enough background about his predecessor's "Usher" to make "Usher II" self-explanatory.

POLITICAL BACKGROUND—AND PROPHECY

Writing in 1950 a *Chronicle* supposedly covering events in the year 2005, Bradbury has his protagonist, William Stendhal, "look back" to the political and cultural repression in America that supposedly culminated in the "Great Fire," "The Burning" (of books) in 1975. Actually, Bradbury was simply extrapolating from the political situation he knew well in 1950, at the dawn of what would later be called the Age of McCarthyism. Many unscrupulous politicians succeeded in those days in silencing public figures they disagreed with simply by accusing them of "communism" or treason. For example, Richard Nixon would later admit that he had won his first election to Congress by calling his opponent a communist even though he knew she wasn't! Many writers, publishers, performers, librarians, and teachers, afraid of losing their livelihood, were intimidated into expressing only "safe" views—or no political views at all. As Bradbury's Stendhal says, the word "politics" became a synonym for communism, "and it was worth your life to use the word!"

In his 1967 introduction to the Simon & Schuster edition of *Fahrenheit 451*, Bradbury cited Senator Joseph McCarthy as one of the three greatest bookburners, along with Hitler and the Chinese Red Guard. Although Senator McCarthy was condemned by the United States Senate in 1954, some aspects of McCarthyism have actually persisted in American life until— and well past-Bradbury's "1975." For example, PEN American Center is constantly defending writers and publishers whose books have been banned in certain localities.

Given the climate in 1950, then, we can credit Bradbury with great courage in speaking out against censorship and thus of spurious "anti-Red" tactics. And given the climate today, we can credit him again with the gift of prophecy.

THEMES OF "USHER II"

Repression of the imagination and too much a control over people's lives can result only in severe psychological and social reaction. Humanity is happiest when it is allowed a healthful balance of the rational and the irrational, reason and emotion, logic and imagination. Upsetting that balance is one way to trigger sudden metamorphosis.

LITERARY BACKGROUND: POE'S USHER

Poe's story opens with his narrator pausing outside the "melancholy House of Usher." He has been summoned by his old school friend, Roderick Usher, to help him cope with an exhausting physical and mental illness. The narrator is depressed by the sight of the decaying mansion—its bleak walls discolored with fungi, its windows like vacant eyes, with a strange crack in the structure that makes its way zigzag down the front wall until it becomes "lost in the sullen waters of the tarn." This is a small mountain lake that has no outlets and thus becomes dark and dank from lack of circulation. The narrator stares down into the tarn and sees the mansion mirrored upside down.

"Ushered" by a servant into the presence of Roderick, the narrator finds himself in a dark, cavernous room with tattered furniture, the man himself agitated, in a profound depression. Roderick fears, among other disasters, the death of his only surviving relative, his sister. Madeline suffers from a strange malady that leaves her often in a *cataleptic* state (temporary paralysis).

The narrator and the host pass the time talking, reading, painting, playing music. Roderick accompanies himself on his guitar with songs of his own composition, e.g., with "The Haunted

Palace," a song about a monarch in the Realm of Thought whose mansion is assailed by Evil.

When Madeline dies, Roderick explains they cannot inter her in the family burial ground. One implication is that her body might be stolen and sold as a cadaver to medical students. So they place her in a coffin in a locked vault deep in the cellar.

One night during a violent storm, Roderick, rocking to and fro in his chair, interprets a series of crashing sounds as the escape of his sister from her tomb. Indeed Madeline appears with blood on her shroud, and rushes to embrace Roderick, the two collapsing into death.

The narrator flees in horror and looking back, sees the house collapse along the zigzag crack down into the tarn.

POE AND THE MORAL CLIMATE
"The Fall of the House of Usher" is exactly the kind of imaginative literature that the puritanical bookburners in Bradbury's fictitious "1975" would have had to repress. And one reason Bradbury's protagonist Stendhal would build "Usher II" is that Poe's story tells us exactly what happens when we suppress the imagination. Poe's "Usher I" delivers perfectly the typical underlying message of the Gothic tale.

LITERARY BACKGROUND: THE GOTHIC ROMANCE
This was a kind of fiction that deliberately explored the bizarre, the grotesque, the noncivilized, subjective, and irrational aspects of life. Why? Gothic fiction was an answer to the Age of Reason, with its emphasis on the logical, orderly, objective, civilized aspects. Romanticists like Poe were interested in compensating for the neoclassicist repression of the irrational and the subjective. This perfectly suits Bradbury's needs in a story about Stendhal's rebellion against the highly repressive world of 2005.

As the critic Syndy McMillen Conger explains it, the relationship of the Gothic romance to society is captured in Poe's image of the dank tarn. Like the tarn, the Gothic tale does mirror reality, but it also turns it upside down so that the hidden, dark side can also be seen.

LITERARY BACKGROUND: PSYCHOLOGY AND POE

It is no coincidence then that interest in Gothic fiction thrives in the twentieth century, the age of Freudian analysis of the irrational. A Freudian might see Roderick as exemplifying the Ego, struggling to repress (bury!) his own passions, the Id, as symbolized by Madeline. Or another psychological critic might need the House as the mind of the narrator, in which his conscious and unconscious struggle for supremacy. Poe himself said, in a letter, that the Haunted House is meant to be "a mind haunted by phantoms." Still another critic interprets the action this way: Because of his close association with Roderick, the narrator himself is tipped over into madness. The weird ending then is his hallucination.

OTHER SYMBOLISM IN "USHER I"

The Ushers live in isolation. They do not circulate in the world. They stagnate like the tarn which symbolizes their stasis and desuetude. The crack in the facade may also symbolize this or some other fatal flaws in their makeup.

SUGGESTIVENESS

Critics of all schools are concerned with certain unanswered questions. Did Roderick deliberately or unwittingly bury his sister alive? What was the great secret Roderick was afraid to share with his friend? Was it that he and his sister have committed—or have fought the urge to commit—incest? But on the psychological level that would mean they had fought against the union of the Ego and the Id, a self-destructive struggle. How did Madeline escape her locked coffin and locked tomb? Did the storm crack open first the cellar where she was entombed and then the whole building? Unanswered questions are a characteristic of Romanticism, which prefers suggestiveness to solid statement.

BRADBURY'S SETTING: TWO POE TALES

It makes sense then that Stendhal, given wealth that can afford any reprisal against the repressive establishment, would want, defiantly, to rebuild the House of Usher and use it as the symbolic place in which he deals symbolically with his enemies: the Society for the Prevention of Fantasy and the United States Department of Moral Climates.

The quotation with which Stendhal opens the story is the opening sentence of Poe's tale, and the passage that Pikes recites as Usher II sinks into the tarn is Poe's closing sentence. The details of the exterior of the House, and of the grounds—at least those details which the architect Bigelow checks over carefully with Stendhal—are all drawn from Poe's "Usher."

The interior, however, is modeled after the palace of Prince Prospero in Poe's "The Masque of the Red Death." The Prince stages a ball in a suite of seven rooms, each one a different color. If Bradbury's Inspector Garrett of Moral Climates, and the Society officials, had known their Poe, they would have trembled at the very thought of dancing in such a suite—where all will die at midnight. The robot rats (with robot fleas!) that scurry through the House are also allusions to the spectre of the "Red Death," which appeared at Prospero's ball. Red Death was a variant of Black Death (bubonic plague) transmitted to man by the fleas carried by rats. And the Red Death is the last robot that we see in "Usher II," also modeled on Poe's death symbol.

THE ACTION: OTHER POE TALES

The major steps in Bradbury's plot are also modeled on still other Poe tales. The dancing seems to produce a pounding beat that a Poe reader would recognize as really coming from under the floor, as in Poe's "The Telltale Heart." The robot ape that kills Miss Blunt and stuffs her body up the chimney is modeled after the ourang-outang in Poe's "The Murders in the Rue Morgue." The razor-sharp pendulum that slices into Mr. Steffens is modeled after the Inquisition machine Poe described in his "The Pit and the Pendulum." Miss Drummond, nailed into a coffin white still alive, of course recalls Poe's "The Premature Burial." And the death that Stendhal reserves for the archvillain, Garrett, is a detailed reenactment of the way Poe's Montresor bricks up a wall around his enemy, Fortunato, in "The Cask of Amontillado."

LITERARY BACKGROUND: CHILDREN'S TALES

Fairy-tale robots mingling with Stendhal's guests are all reminders of fantasy literature now (2005) banned by the repressive American government. Tweedledee and Tweedledum, Mock Turtle, and Doormouse are characters from Lewis Carroll's (Charles Lutwidge Dodgson's) *Alice in Wonderland* and *Through the Looking Glass*. Tik-Tok is the protagonist of Frank Baum's *Tik-Tok of Oz*; St. Nicholas, of course, is the Dutch original of Santa Claus; and Bluebeard is the wife-killer first described by Charles Perrault in his 1703 volume of fairy tales. And the robot Rapunzel, who lets down her hair so the guests can climb into the House, is a character from *Grimm's Fairy Tales*.

LITERARY BACKGROUND: CLASSICS DESTROYED

In his effort to impress us with the enormity of bookburning, Bradbury has Stendhal recite to Bigelow the names of other American authors (besides Poe) burned in "1975," as well as the names of some of the lovable characters who were "executed." Nathaniel Hawthorne (1804–1864) was a writer of romances who often used science for its symbolic value (symbolic of man's curiosity and the evil it can provoke; this theme is related to Bradbury's in "The Million-Year Picnic"). Ambrose Bierce (1842–1914) left behind twelve volumes of stories and aphorisms; sardonic in style, he dwelt on the macabre and the mystifying in everyday life. H. P. Lovecraft (1890–1937) wrote fiction that intensively explores our fear of the unknown.

The fictional characters that the Moral Climates people have removed from human experience thirty years before 2005 include readers' favorites from Washington Irving (the Headless Horseman is from his "Legend of Sleepy Hollow"), Frank Baum

(Glinda the Good is from his *Wizard of Oz*), and Wilhelm and Jakob Grimm (Snow White and Rumpelstiltskin are from *Grimm's Fairy Tales*).

HEMINGWAY AS A SYMBOL

Stendhal uses Ernest Hemingway (1899–1961) as symbolic of the dominance of realism in American literature. In early work especially, Hemingway wrote in a highly controlled, stoic, objective, macho style that influenced a whole generation of writers.

BACKGROUND: THE BURNING CREWS

"Usher II" is one of three works published in 1950 in which Bradbury uses his ironic concept of "The Fireman" as a public official who starts fires. Galaxy published Bradbury's story by that name (later to be expanded into *Fahrenheit 451*) in which firemen cleanse the community by burning books. And firemen who sanitize Mars for the Americans by burning the remains of Martians are expected soon in "The Musicians," one of the chronicles for 2003.

AUTOBIOGRAPHICAL ELEMENTS

A traumatic experience of Bradbury's boyhood was his discovery of a wall of flame in his grandparents' house. Fire became, in his adult writings, a malevolent force, symbolic of human evil.

CHARACTERIZATION: TAG NAMES

Bradbury does not use tag names very often. But he makes excellent use of them here. He gives his protagonist the name *Stendhal*, pseudonym of the French author Marie Henri Beyle (1783–1842). Why? Probably because Stendhal's heroes are passionate and energetic, live by their own moral code, and find happiness in passionate love or the energetic use of power. This description suits William Stendhal and his values perfectly.

For Stendhal's assistant, Bradbury uses the name *Pikes*. A pike is a military spear. Pikes seems to bristle with spears and certainly he spears his enemies on this fateful night.

Bradbury gives his villain the name of *Garrett*. This is pronounced just as though it were "garret," a word of a room at the top of the house, or for a turret or watchtower. All these meanings can apply to the Inspector of Moral Climates. In the Freudian imagery of the mind, the garret or watchtower would be the home of the Superego which, like Garrett, tries to repress the imagination. Note that Stendhal chooses the cellar, the dwelling place of the irrational Unconscious, as the ironic setting of Garrett's demise.

The name of the Society for the Prevention of Fantasy is modeled on the name of the *American Society for the Prevention of Cruelty to Animals* (ASPCA). The ironic implication is that fantasy is cruel to humans and should be prevented. One of the Society's officials is named Blunt: as an adjective this can mean "dull, slow to understand;" as a verb, "to make less sensitive or emotional," which certainly is what the Society wants to do to the citizenry.

CHARACTERIZATION: THE CONFORMISTS
They are timid. The officials of the Society for the Prevention of Fantasy did not dare come to Mars until the more energetic and adventurous pioneers had made it a safe place. (So we learned in the prelude to "Usher II," "The Naming of Names.") Now that Mars has been "civilized," i.e., Americanized, the conformists come to impose their own standards on—to regulate the lives of—the passionate and the daring.

CHARACTER OF BIGELOW
Bigelow the architect is a man in conflict between conformity and nonconformity. In his own field, he has been excited by the great opportunity that Stendhal's project has given him to be daring, innovative, nonconformist. He admits that without Stendhal's private rockets he would "never have been allowed to bring most of the equipment through." So he has dared do

something illegal. But outside his field, he plays it safe. So far as he has heard, "the Burning was a good thing." Bradbury reveals here one of the tragedies of political repression: the timid endure it by compartmentalizing their lives.

CHARACTERIZATION: GARRETT

Garrett represents the kind of person who can concentrate his originality on style because he does not have to worry about originality in the content of his life; that he takes readymade from the authorities. He outsmarts Stendhal by sending a robot of himself the first time, and he enjoys making the ironic remark that you can't depend on robots: "Other people's . . . especially." But Bradbury's characterization here is perfect in its irony of the tragic. It's Garrett's ignorance of Poe's "Cask of Amontillado" that traps him. He sees other Poe tales being reenacted. But he does not see "The Cask" unfolding, as he descends, plied with liquor, into the catacombs. Stendhal drives home the point: he is punishing Garrett for not first having read the books he burned. Bradbury's allusion here is to those many censors (of, say, Kurt Vonnegut's *Slaughterhouse Five* or Mark Twain's *Huckleberry Finn*, banned in many school and public libraries) who act simply on hearsay evidence. The bishop who condemned a play by William Butler Yeats did so without having read or seen it: he replied on a summary of the plot provided by others. Stendhal is punishing such people for not thinking for themselves.

CHARACTERIZATION: PIKES

Bradbury uses four methods of characterizing Pikes:

> 1. He describes Pikes as seen by another person, Stendhal, his boss.

> 2. He makes Pikes's genius clear by contrasting him with other geniuses. Lon Chaney (1883–1930), the great pantomimist and makeup artist, the great performer in monster movies, was known as "the man of 1000 faces." But Stendhal thinks of Pikes as "the man of 10,000 faces." He's greater even than Boris Karloff (1887–1969) and

Bela Lugosi (1884–1965), other geniuses in monster roles. These last two, incidentally, played in The Black Cat; Pikes's robots out on the dance floor incline Black Cats.

3. Bradbury is careful to make Pikes human by giving him the deepest, most tragic and demonic motivation: the need for revenge, in this case, revenge this night for the night that the authorities burned his films.

4. Bradbury fills the stage with Pikes's creations, who remind us minute-by-minute of the genius and thoroughness of their maker.

CHARACTERIZATION: STENDHAL

The protagonist of "Usher II" is one of Bradbury's finest creations, surely one of the twentieth century's greatest characters in the short story format. He is the equivalent in the SF short story of Captain Nemo in the SF novel. He has the imagination, the creativity, the passion to strike back against repression with finesse, panache, verve. He is masterful in detailed planning and timing. But when one of his plans goes awry—and Garrett does detect that it's a different robot that rockets back—Stendhal is still able to handle the now-more-dangerous situation. He is that rarity: a cultured intellectual who can function well in the world of power struggles. Notice that he is proud to have "nurtured a medieval atmosphere" in the world of Cleanminded modernists. He knows his literature well enough to know that the Gothic tale is medieval in character, and in its opposition to neoclassicism. His motivation is both personal and social: Revenge for his own 50,000-book library destroyed by the Burning Crew; revenge on the "antiseptic government" for its repression of the imagination.

AUTOBIOGRAPHICAL ELEMENTS

Stendhal is modeled partly on Bradbury. Before he could read, he was taken frequently to the movies by his mother; his aunt read him *The Wizard of Oz* when he was six; throughout boyhood and adolescence he haunted the library. Stendhal's passion for the products of the imagination is Bradbury's own.

SCIENCE FICTION

The plastics and the robots that make "Usher II" possible are much more advanced than those available when Bradbury wrote the story in 1950, indeed, more advanced than we have four decades later, when we boast that "robots can now guide a brain surgeon's probe with unsurpassed accuracy" (David Moberg, "The Robotics Industry," *In These Times*, May 13–19, 1987). And in response to Touponce, that critic who sees only one resemblance of Bradbury's Mars to science's Mars, we should add another (our fifth) resemblance. As we discover in "Usher II," Mars—because it is a tilted planet with a long elliptical orbit—has definite seasons.

SENSUOUS DETAIL AND METAPHOR

Bradbury's imagery is superlative in this one-of-his-best tales. Again and again he forces us to make surprising connections. The grass on the grounds of Usher II is *raven grass*. That is, it looks like the lustrous black feathers the raven sports. The robots are covered with silks the color of frog and fern. We learn that nostrils too can wink! We see Bluebeard's whiskers in an entirely new way: they are like acetylene flame. And, as if to cap Poe's "odor of the sharp steel" ("The Pit and the Pendulum"), Bradbury has us note the *smell of . . . lathed brass*. Perhaps Bradbury's strongest simile in this story comes in Stendhal's thinking about the night they seized Pikes's films, *like entrails yanked from the camera*.

APOSTROPHE

Bradbury also uses effectively here another figure of speech, one not used much today: the *apostrophe*. This is a speech delivered to someone who is not present. Bradbury has carefully prepared us for such an emotional outlet before Stendhal warns the unseen rockets that he'll teach their passengers a lesson for what they did to Poe.

IRONY

The figure of speech Bradbury uses most often in "Usher II" is irony, or the literary play on the differences between the appearance and the reality. Garrett first sees Stendhal as "a small" man, ironic when we discover his real, portentous size. Is it also part of Bradbury's motivation that Stendhal, like Napoleon, overcompensates for his smallness by flaunting his greatness? Garrett is frightened by an ape, is reassured that it's only a robot, then suffers from it anyhow. Stendhal and Pikes think they have killed the real Garrett but they've only burned his robot. The guests first think they're seeing the real Ms. Blunt getting murdered, and then believe-as we do-that only her robot-look-alike is dead, whereas the first possibility proves correct after all.

Irony galvanizes speech after speech. "You'll be burning Babbitts next!" Stendhal tells Garrett. That means nothing to the uncultured Garrett, but to us it is highly ironic: Sinclair Lewis's novel Babbitt (hence our word babbittry) portrays Babbitt as the ultimate conformist, but because he's a literary creation, Stendhal is really saying, you'll burn him too. Again, when Garrett shouts "Murder," and Stendhal replies "Murder most foul," Garrett cannot know what we know: those are the words of King Hamlet's ghost! The ultimate irony in "Usher II," of course, inheres in the reality that for all his boasting of his familiarity with Poe, Garrett does not know enough to save himself from the "Amontillado" trap. "I'm being ironic," Stendhal tells Garrett as he bricks him in.

POINT OF VIEW
Bradbury uses here his favorite point of view: that of the author as limited narrator. In this case, he limits himself and us to reality as perceived by William Stendhal. Since here the point-of-view character survives, there is no last-minute switch in the camera angle, as we had in "The Third Expedition" and "The Earth Men."

IMPORTANCE
This story, we said at the beginning of our discussion of "Usher II," ranks high as science fantasy, as a horror story, as black humor, and as a dystopian work. The events in "Usher II"—from the burning of all imaginative literature to Stendhal's revenge—would be painful to contemplate except that Bradbury

makes each event absurd and ironic. Still, like all black humor (e.g., Joseph Heller's *Catch-22*), "Usher II" leaves us with a bitter message.

Fiction about an ideal, good place is called utopian (after Sir Thomas More's 1516 novel *Utopia*). Fiction about some distant or future society where "progress" has backfired (as in Aldous Huxley's *Brave New World*) is called dystopian. Surely the latter is true of "Usher II," and of the *Chronicles* generally.

PART 5

AUGUST 2005: THE OLD ONES

FUNCTION

To indicate how really safe and "civilized" Mars is now, Bradbury adds to his earlier "waves" of explorers, pioneers, settlers, and sophisticates a new group: retirees. This tiny interchapter, a perfect example of Bradbury's poetic prose style, also serves to set the stage for the next full story, "The Martian," in which the point-of-view character and his wife are "old ones."

CHARACTERIZATION

Instead of describing these retirees as "physically failing" and "economically middle-class," Bradbury characterizes them through revealing details: dry and crackling, with wry mouths, they take their pulse regularly; they are people who travel long distances in "chair cars," i.e., railroad cars with no sleeping accommodations.

METAPHORIC EPITHETS

The passage culminates in two shocking epithets that serve also as metaphors: the *mummy* people both names and describes them as looking dried-up but well-preserved; the *dried-apricot* people not only names them as persons obliged to eat laxative fruits, but also once again describes the color and texture of their skin.

DICTION AND SYNTAX

We have made this passage our main example of Bradbury's "Sentence Maneuvers" in Chapter 4.

SEPTEMBER 2005: THE MARTIAN

FREUDIAN SCIENCE FICTION

This story is SF to the extent that psychology is a science, and it is Freudian in at least one important way. It was Freud's premise that dreams, fantasies, and hence art itself are forms of wish-fulfillment or expressions of anxiety. Both sources of dream states are exploited in "The Martian."

T-S-H

In discussing earlier stories we noted that Bradbury gives to some Martians certain powers of telepathy, hypnosis, and projections of ideas into solid existence. Now we should note that sometimes these selected Martians are in active control of the effects of T-S-H, as in "The Third Expedition." In that story the Martians delude Earth men into seeing what they want to see: Mars as Heaven, with their dead relatives alive and happy in a town that seems to be a reconstruction of Green Bluff, Illinois. But other times the Martians are in a state of passive reception of the results of their own T-S-H. Thus, in "Ylla" and "The Summer Night," certain sensitive Martians suffer as receivers of mental influences from approaching Earth men that they—the sensitive Martians—cannot cope with.

Although Bradbury has not made this explicit, one basic premise seems to be that when the Martians are in the majority and can take the initiative in a situation they can prepare for (as in The Third Expedition), they can then exert mental control over humans. But when they are in a minority, surrounded by humans (as in "The Martian"—note the singular), and taken unawares, their T-S-H may go out of control.

PREMISES APPLIED

Thus, the lone Martian in the story can cope with circumstances when he deals with one or two persons and is prepared for them. He rather involuntarily reads their minds and changes his appearance to fulfill their wishes: in the case of the old LaFarge couple, that they have their dead boy Tom back with them; in the case of the Spauldings, their missing daughter Lavinia. So, too, the Martian may read a mind and realize its worst anxiety: in the case of the murderer Nomland, the Martian becomes the murdered Gillings come back to haunt Nomland. Only Nomland's suicide, apparently, saves the Martian from being trapped in the Gillings role. But when the Martian is greatly outnumbered and numerous conflicting wishes are released on him—that he be a husband returned to a deserted wife, a fugitive found by a policeman, a Tom or Lavinia found again—the lone Martian, pulled in many directions, disintegrates.

CHARACTERIZATION: THE MARTIAN

This situation is rife for complex character development. Although the Martian is forced simultaneously into several roles and comes to a tragic end, the point-of-view character, "Lafe" LaFarge, grows as a result of his experience with "Tom and Lavinia." The Martian is a poignantly sympathetic character whom SF aficionados love the way film buffs love *E.T.* Bradbury provides almost hour-by-hour motivation for the Martian's conduct during the last twenty-four hours of his life. It's his loneliness, his need for living companionship, that drives him to stake his life on the chance the LaFarges will accommodate his needs. So long as he can control their perception of him, he is safe and happy as barefoot Tom returned. But Bradbury designs two plot developments that put the Martian in peril. When Lafe insists on knowing the truth, Tom must leave; apparently, only as Tom does he have any claim on the LaFarge's hospitality. But when he is almost trapped in the Gillings role, he returns hoping now that his "father" can accept him as he is: a facsimile of his son, good for his "mother's" morale. LaFarge's understanding at this point is the first step he takes toward becoming a bigger person, intellectually and emotionally. But now it's the mother who endangers the Martian. Her insistence that they spend a night on the town puts him into the perilous situation explored above: a telepathichypnotic

Martian surrounded by many humans with strong wishes and fears.

CONFLICT AND CRISIS

Bradbury stages a powerful crisis-to-climax scene. Out on a balcony, away from the Spauldings' direct perception of him as their Lavinia, the Martian is torn by internal, ethical conflict: he has a choice of hurting either the Spauldings or Mrs. La-Farge. But Mr. LaFarge is very much there, exerting direct perception of the Martian as their son, and so the Martian's mind is recaptured by the people he seems to prefer anyway (is it because they live on the outskirts of town, where humans are less numerous?). Too many external conflicts have been set in motion, however, and he is the victim of the psychological crossfire. The scene in which his identity changes every few seconds as the crowd express their individual hopes and fears is a natural for the cinema and is well done in the 1980 teleplay.

"THE MARTIAN" AS ALLEGORY

One reason the Martian gains our sympathy is that he becomes an allegorical figure for the personality that tries to be what others want him to be. Since we all, to some extent, are forced to adjust to life in just that way, we can all identify with him. Our interest in him is further heightened by imagining our own private wishes and fears externalized where everybody can see them.

CHARACTERIZATION: LAFE

Mr. LaFarge undergoes profound character change. It's his longing for Tom that assigns the lonely Martian at the door a human role. But it's LaFarge's indifference to the Martian as a Martian that drives him away. Yet, by the time Tom returns from his Gillings scare, Lafe has begun to love him as he is: a Martian and a replacement for Tom. And when LaFarge vies for the Martian (now Lavinia) on the balcony, he promises the Martian everything he needs; and LaFarge deliberately exerts his willpower over the Martian to help him metamorphose back into Tom. LaFarge thus becomes the second human

(Gomez was the first) to understand the Martian psyche and deliberately to interact with it.

CHARACTERIZATION: ANNA

Mrs. LaFarge is a pathetic character whose need to dominate has brought new tragedy to the family. At the beginning, she insists Lafe forget all about Tom. Yet, later, she is the parent more involved emotionally with the Martian facsimile, although her love for her son is possessive. She overrides the boy's preference for staying at home as well as Lafe's siding with the boy. Her lack of curiosity about the Martian's fear of town brings to the LaFarges a second death of a dependent child.

SETTING

Note that Bradbury here combines his Lowellian canal-scape with a rough frontier town of the Old West variety, with its boisterous drunks and piano-playing in the saloon. This setting makes it not at all unusual that killer Nomland is at large and Spaulding tries to settle a dispute between families with a gun.

THEMES

We can see, then, that "The Martian" is still another dramatization of Bradbury's two major themes: metamorphosis, as reflected in the characterizations of LaFarge and his facsimile son; and the effect of subjective states on perception of objective reality, as shown in the different ways the human characters perceive the Martian.

POINT OF VIEW

Bradbury relates "The Martian" from the point of view of the author as limited narrator. What we know and discover is limited to what Mr. LaFarge sees, perceives, and thinks; the action follows him and occurs only in his presence. Other stories told in this manner so far have been "Ylla," "The Green Morning," and "Usher II." Still four other stories have been told from the same point of view but with at least one shift in the point-of-view character: "The Earth Men," "The Third Expedition," "—And the Moon Be Still as Bright," and "Night Meeting."

NOVEMBER 2005: THE LUGGAGE STORE

STRUCTURAL FUNCTION

This interchapter signals the second turning point in the action, which is divided into four sections. The first section of *Chronicles*—from "Rocket Summer" to "The Third Expedition"—concerns the expeditions that fail. "—And the Moon Be Still as Bright" signaled the first turning point, when expeditions began to take hold. From that story on through "The Martian," the second section of *Chronicles* has recorded a continuous buildup of migrations to and settlement on Mars. But with "The Luggage Store," the movement is reversed. The third section will deal with the sudden abandonment of Mars and mass return to the homeland, because it is endangered by nuclear war. The fourth section—"The Million-Year Picnic"—is an epilogue. The full rationale of this structure is discussed in Chapter 4, "Plot Structure, Techniques, and Style."

"The Luggage Store" is properly classified as an interchapter because it gives us an overview of the general situation in Mars-Earth relations. Even though it has two characters, one even individualized with a name, they are not developed and so this piece does not qualify as a story.

SOCIAL PSYCHOLOGY AND HISTORY

The luggage-store owner's explanation of why the settlers will return *en masse* sounds plausible: they haven't been on Mars long enough to feel separated from their now-endangered relatives and native land. But history makes that explanation sound incomplete and shallow. Centuries after Englishmen had settled Canada, Australia, and New Zealand, they still—in World Wars I and II—returned by the hundreds of thousands to support the English homeland. Psychology also demands a fuller explanation. The full truth includes the long-standing American tendency to violate virgin territory and move on, because there's always another place to start over in. Bradbury's *Chronicles*, in effect, have extended that practice from the American West to the Red Planet. In "The Luggage Store," the restless Americans are seen once again as ready to pull up stakes and get a move on, even if that means moving back: so long as it's on to new excitement: the war provides the perfect rationale.

TAG NAME

Bradbury, as we've noted before in "Usher II," seldom uses tag names but when he does, he does it well. And so Father Peregrine, the first customer to buy a "new valise" in the "rush sale" the owner has predicted, becomes also a symbolic customer. For the word peregrine means roving, migratory; to peregrinate means to journey from place to place; peregrinism is the tendency to wander. Bradbury's dubbing the customer Peregrine supports the ideas offered above.

"THE MESSIAH"

Indeed, Father Peregrine has *peregrinated* out of two of Bradbury's separate Martian stories, in which he is the main character, into the *Chronicles*, where he becomes a symbolic walk-on. In "Fire Balloons," a delightful and brilliant work, Peregrine raises the question of whether the clergy should expect to find Martians with more than five senses (ten maybe?) and what the theological implications would be. On Mars he finds out. One race of Martians, the Fire Balloons, have so many senses they don't need to go to church to be moral and ethical! In "The Messiah," Peregrine, whose deepest wish of course is to see the Lord Jesus face-to-face, glances at a Martian who comes into his church and sees the Martian as the Christ! This scene was worked into the 1980 teleplay. "The Fire Balloons" was added to the 1973 hardcover edition of the *Chronicles*, now out of print.

SETTING AND SYMBOLISM

Bradbury has chosen a luggage shop, symbolic of *peregrinism*, as the setting for the symbolic customer's decision to resume his peregrinations.

NOVEMBER 2005: THE OFF SEASON

FIRST TWO WORDS: LINKAGE

"Sam Parkhill," Bradbury's first two words in "The Off Season," link it at once to the earlier tale "—And the Moon Be Still as Bright." Parkhill is the last name we read in "Moon," which ended with Captain Wilder's knocking Parkhill's teeth out because he was shattering the Martians' crystal windows with rifle bullets. In "The Off Season," then, Sam comes to us already characterized as a despoiler. Remember, it was he who wanted to splash Spender's head all over Mars. The two stories both appeared originally as magazine pieces in 1948.

IRONY: LINKAGE

From his early linking of the two stories, right through to the end of this social satire, Bradbury revels in irony. One form of irony results when a character says more than he realizes. Thus, the reader can appreciate a pun that Bradbury puts into Sam's mouth but that Sam himself does not "get." Wilder, Sam tells his wife, has been sent on a rocket to Jupiter. "They kicked him upstairs." This expression describes one way to get rid of someone: promote him to a higher but ineffectual post. But Wilder has also literally been sent up the stairs into Outer Space, from the third planet (Earth) and the fourth (Mars) to the fifth (Jupiter).

Thus, Bradbury again dramatizes the fate of the dissenter (consider the fate of the Taxpayer, Spender, Stendhal, Pikes). And Sam's pleasure at Wilder's twenty-year exile "for shooting off his mouth" of course further characterizes Sam as a conformist and Wilder as having kept his promise—to speak out for Spender's ideas. (Do you think Sam has ever told his wife the truth about why he now wears false teeth?)

CHARACTERIZATION: THE MARTIANS

Bradbury characterizes the Martians in two ways:

> 1. He lets us hear Sam's and Elma's views of the Martians. Sam's view is as much a characterization of himself as it is of the Martians. He doesn't like strangers and it shows in his trigger-happy uneasiness. (We are reminded that Sam's old crewmate, Spender, said that anything "strange" is "no good" to an American.) Sam sees the

Martians as weirdly uncivilized because they wander about, have no leaders and no laws. (To the white man, the Indians also seemed to be rootless, leaderless, lawless, although in fact their tribal customs imposed a strong moral code on their behavior.) Worst of all, to Sam, they won't accept defeat and get out of his way. He is so stubbornly convinced of their irrelevance, he won't listen even when they tell him they have important news about Earth! And at the end he considers them stupid because they haven't exacted vengeance on him when they had the clear advantage of numbers and position. Because he himself is bloodthirsty (remember how he wanted to shoot Spender in the head so as to splash his brains about?), he cannot conceive of a genuinely pacifist people. Even if he had heard Spender say they were ("Wars ceased," he told Wilder), Sam wouldn't be able to comprehend it.

2. The author also lets us ourselves observe the Martians. As we see for ourselves, they actually do "turn the other cheek" on each of the occasions in which Sam kills a Martian emissary. Spender has already told us that their civilization outgrew war in order to live for the sake of living. (But they have not, apparently, outgrown crimes of passion; remember Yll?)

But why do they give Sam land grants for half of Mars? This action seems to have developed from their telepathic interception of radio messages from an American station on Mars. Do they wish to offer the settlers all that space to accommodate refugees from the Earth war they know (and Sam doesn't) has just begun? Are the grants made in the hope that this way the Martians can keep the other half? If so, they should tune in on some American Indian tribes who tried that approach in making innumerable solemn treaties, all of them broken by Sam's grandfathers and great-grandfathers. Are they, out of nobility, giving this territory to the Parkhills as a consolation for the loss of Earth? Or do they, seeing their own decline, want to make sure that other intelligent life still has a place for survival after the war on Earth?

Bradbury makes it clear that to him, the Martians are beautiful and graceful people: he lavishes gorgeous similes on them. The first Martian emissary that Sam kills collapses slowly like a stately tent. Twice Bradbury uses multiple similes in their behalf. the second emissary impresses herself on Sam like breath, like smoke, like lace, like a snowflake, like icy rime (frost). And when the Martian sandships sail off, Bradbury can describe their movements only by invoking comparisons with petals, plumes, butterflies, moon thistles.

CHARACTERIZATION: SAM

So far we have seen Sam as a despoiler; a conformist in a despoiler society; a *xenophobe* (one who compulsively hates strangers); prone to settling things recklessly and unjustly with a gun; oblivious that the Martians might have something to offer him, something he can learn from them; contemptuous of them because they haven't killed him after he slew two of them. You have doubtless noticed that Sam is also greedy. Bradbury sums up Sam's greediness in an extraordinary burst of irony. Once again, Bradbury's fiction makes artistic use of allusion to poetry.

On the pedestal of the Statue of Liberty, in New York harbor, there is engraved a five-line passage from Emma Lazarus's sonnet "The New Colossus," meaning the statue itself, which speaks:

> Give me your tired, your poor,
> Your huddled masses yearning to breathe free,
> The wretched refuse of your teeming shore,
> Send them, the homeless, tempest tossed, to me:
> I lift my lamp beside the golden door.

Now Sam, thinking of his hotdog stand built at a Mars crossroads, thinking of the thousands of new migrants expected any hour now, experiences a great burst of patriotism. But he can only remember this garbled line:

> Send me your hungry and your starved . . .

so that, of course, he can rake in the profits. His identification of patriotism with slobbering greed, of himself with Lady Liberty, is not to be missed. Of course, if he were a better informed xenophobe, Sam wouldn't remember Emma Lazarus's poetry at all—she was Jewish.

CHARACTERIZATION: ELMA

She seems to have a better sense of the Martian mood than he does. She does not panic in three confrontations with Martians, actually faces the situation more courageously than he, and scorns him for his rash conduct. However, she seems to feel no real sympathy for the murdered people either. Apparently, she has long been able to shame him for his crude blunders. Twice, she seems ready to be separated from him, and has to be dragged along or kept by force and threats. Near the end, she seems totally detached from him. She comes to life again— and this is probably Bradbury's most sardonic picture of spitefulness—only when she sees nuclear explosions on Earth and realizes what it means for Sam's hotdog trade. Again, she seems to have no real sympathy for the victims of violence. Instead, she actually revels in the realization that Sam's business, even before it opens, suffers an "off season."

PARALLELS TO UNITED STATES HISTORY

The white man's treatment of the Martians, as we've already hinted, repeats the Americans' treatment of the Indians. There is a less obvious parallel in Elma's talking about "work rockets" coming up with 100,000 Mexicans and Chinese. This would repeat two other dark dramas in American history. The United States imported large groups of poor Chinese to build western railroads under appalling living conditions and for low—"coolie"—wages. The United States for decades now has used cheap, temporary, migratory labor from Mexico to reap the harvest—at "peon" wages—for American farmers.

DICTION

Bradbury's colorful vocabulary, and his artistic use of it, account for much of the rich texture of his fiction. Here are some examples from "The Off Season:"

preening—A bird is preening when it smoothes or cleans its feathers with its beak or bill. Bradbury uses the word to describe the action of the sharp prows of the sandships on the dead-sea bottom.

keening—This is a wailing for the dead. Bradbury uses the word to describe the sound a Martian ship makes as it speeds over the sand.

flinders—Bradbury could have said that Sam's bullets tear the Martian tower to bits, fragments, splinters. Instead, he uses a more colorful synonym, flinders.

soldiering—Congratulating himself on having left the service, Sam ridicules his old buddies who are "soldiering around still." But Bradbury plants the word here with its second meaning shining through: deliberately working slowly, loafing surreptitiously, "goldbricking."

The Disease—Bradbury's creatures on Mars have narrowed down the meaning of the word to signify just one sickness: the smallpox that Americans carry to Mars and that kills off the Martians.

THEMES

In his *The Bradbury Chronicles*, George Edgar Slusser sums up "The Off Season" this way: "Parkhill, of the original spoilers of Mars, is in turn spoiled by Earth." You could call that poetic justice. Human aggressiveness has brought tragedy to intelligent life simultaneously on both Earth and on its colonized Red Planet, another version of Bradbury's concern with unintended metamorphosis.

POINT OF VIEW

At first glance, we might say Bradbury writes here as the author as *limited narrator*, limited here to the point of view of Sam Parkhill. But on closer study we see that Bradbury never really takes us inside Sam's head. So, actually, this is our second example of Bradbury's writing as the author as *objective narrator*, outside everybody. (See also our section on "Way in the Middle of the Air" in this chapter, and "Point of View" in Chapter 4.)

PART 6

NOVEMBER 2005: THE WATCHER

TIME OVERLAP AND ZOOM BACK

In "The Off Season," we were with the Martians when they already knew about the war on Earth, and with the Parkhills when they saw a blowup on Earth so big that it could be seen forty million miles away. We saw the sardonic meaning of that explosion for one couple. Now, in this interchapter, Bradbury does something usual by pulling back for an overview, but along with an unusual use of time-overlap. He goes back in time (an hour or so?) to see how most Americans on Mars react to the radio news about "the coming war" on the home planet. Then he gives us a more detailed run-through of the atomic explosion and carries the action beyond it.

TIME AS SYMBOL

Notice that the last three pieces—"The Luggage Store," "The Off Season," and now "The Watchers"—are all set in November 2005. Just as April usually connotes rebirth and beginning, so "sombre November" (as T. S. Eliot dubs it in *Murder in the Cathedral*) symbolizes the dying of the year, the end.

LINKAGE

"The Watchers" is linked in detail then not only to "The Off Season," but also to "The Luggage Store," as the "rush sale" predicted in that interlude becomes a reality in this one.

GRIM WARNING

Ever since the United States (and later the USSR) started stockpiling nuclear weapons, humanity has feared an accidental firing. With the "premature explosion" of a stockpile that destroys Australia, Bradbury is one of the first writers to put this grim possibility into artistic fiction. Note, too, that he cites his own city of Los Angeles as the first to be deliberately bombed.

DECEMBER 2005: THE SILENT TOWNS

DETAILS EXPLICIT, GENERALIZATION IMPLICIT

As we noted, in the interchapter "The Old Ones," Bradbury described their health—both physical and economic—only by giving significant details that led us, as readers, to formulate for ourselves the abstract thought: "they are physically failing and economically in the lower middle class." "The Silent Towns" is a more elaborate example of Bradbury's mastery of the same technique. We are led ourselves to realize—from such details as cash registers left open and full of money, water running in the tubs, doors left unlocked—just how quickly the Americans boarded rockets for Earth.

"DON'T TELL, SHOW"

Another technique Bradbury uses is to dramatize Walter Gripp's loneliness by having him act out not only his own part as a customer in a restaurant or drug store, but also the part of the waiter and the pharmacist. Bradbury makes Gripp's condition evident not by stating it, but by demonstrating it. Don't tell, as they say in creative-writing classes, but show.

SF

Bradbury here anticipates one of the most useful inventions still to come at the time of his writing (1946–1950): the answering machine. Only instead of our present-day magnetic recorder using magnetic tape, Bradbury's gadget invites the caller to leave a message on "the wire spool." Again, we have "double moonlit silence," another reminder that Bradbury's Mars resembles science's Mars more than Touponce discerned.

BLACK HUMOR

This story is another of Bradbury's sallies into black humor. Walter Gripp's profound misery—as the sole man left on Mars, an Adam who finally contacts the only woman left, only to discover she's unfit to be his Eve—might be unbearable for us if Bradbury had not stressed the comic side of Gripp's predicament.

SUSPENSE

"The Silent Towns" is one of Bradbury's most suspenseful tales as poor Gripp only gradually discovers exactly how telephones might be the way to find another stay-behind.

GRIPP AS MISOGYNIST

At times, the humor becomes unpleasant as Gripp is characterized as a *misogynist* (a woman-hater). Have you missed the cues? For years he has tried to find a quiet, intelligent woman. No luck at all—quite a putdown of the female sex. It means most women are loud and dumb. And Gripp's reasoning on how to reach a woman is also misogynist—e.g., calling luxury hotels because you can leave it to a woman "to put herself up in luxury"—culminating in the decision to concentrate on beauty parlors where his contemptuous approach does discover a woman.

THEMES

Bradbury heightens the suspense by making Genevieve Selsor's voice seductive, so that Walter is in the gripp (is this a tag name?) of a fantasy that makes her totally beautiful. The black humor turns blackest when she proves to be—for him, at least—physically unattractive and psychologically repulsive. Bradbury drives home the theme of fantasy versus reality by having her say that he, too is not quite what she had thought he would be. And after the Americans' almost unanimous decision to return to Earth, one must infer that another theme here is that land-of-origin and relatives-left-behind are their most vital concerns. Or is it that curiosity about the nature of war is irresistible?

AUTHOR AS MISOGYNIST?

That Walter also disappoints Genevieve somewhat comes just in time to save the author from suspicion that he too might be misogynist. After all, before Genevieve—a chocolate-stuffing, chocolate-fingered, chocolate-swollen slob—we've had the cynical, spiteful Elma Parkhill, the domineering, self-centered Anna LaFarge, and the reality that only whores were willing to be the first women on Mars. But we must also remember that Bradbury did create Ylla as a sympathetic character, deserving of a better husband, victimized by patriarchy.

APRIL 2026: THE LONG YEARS

MUSICAL STRUCTURE

Like a composer who explores contrast by following a fast, lively movement with a slow funeral one, Bradbury gives us first a comic story about a man left behind on Mars ("The Silent Towns"), then a tragic tale about another such person ("The Long Years"). The contrast is highlighted when Hathaway, who has yearned for human company for twenty years, learns from Wilder that Gripp, the "Towns" protagonist, enjoys his two-decade-old solitude so much he has refused repatriation to Earth. (The contrast with a female stay-on might have been interesting, but either Wilder's ship has not spotted Genevieve or she burst with obesity.)

LONGEST TIME BREAK

A glance at Bradbury's "Chronology" (table of contents) shows us that the time lapse between "The Silent Towns" and "The Long Years" is the longest break by far between stories in the novel. This is appropriate, psychologically, because it gives the impression of a drawn-out-slowing-down of the action and of a scarcity of events to "chronicle." The break is dictated too by two considerations of plot: 1) Hathaway's solitude would not be so tragic if the interval were much shorter, nor would he have had the time needed to create his masterful facsimiles of his family, or the sounds of a populated town nearby. 2) Also, if Wilder, whose return is foreshadowed in "The Off Season," is indeed to reappear, it cannot be any earlier than

2025, since Parkhill told his wife in 2005 that Wilder's round trip to Jupiter would take twenty years.

LITERARY STRUCTURE

In the best tradition of the well-made story, Bradbury condenses events of twenty years into one continuous twenty-four-hour action. He is able to start so close to the climax because he contrives to handle the preceding 7,300 days in four bursts of flashbacks: Hathaway's reminiscing over his long wait for rescuers; Hathaway's accounting to Wilder of events on Mars since Wilder was "kicked upstairs"; Wilder's accounting to Hathaway of his being out of touch with the war and of finding Gripp 10,000 miles away from the Hathaways' hut; and "Mrs. Hathaway's" recounting for Wilder of her husband's creation and programming of his family of robots.

POINT OF VIEW

Bradbury uses a flexible point of view. First he is the author limited to Hathaway's line of sight; then, the author limited to Wilder's viewpoint; finally, the author omniscient, able to tell us what the four robots are doing long after all human characters have disappeared.

FOUR PHASES OF SUSPENSE

Bradbury's masterfully postponed revelation of Hathaway's secret is sustained through three phases of suspense: the time the reader puzzles over the question alone; the time Wilder and Williamson come, so to speak, to the reader's aid; the time through "Mrs. Hathaway's" detailed explanation. However, a new cause for suspense arises in a fourth phase: How will Wilder and Williamson be able to handle their own "human" involvement with the four Hathaway robots?

Taking just a few examples, notice how Bradbury puzzles us step-by-step. When Hathaway talks to his family, why does Bradbury say they answer "neatly?" When they debate whether war-torn Earth has also become a "tomb planet," why does Bradbury call it a "silent debate?" Is there any connection between the four crosses in the Martian graveyard and the four

"Hathaways" he talks to? Why does he ask the graves for forgiveness? Why, when he asks the four to drink a toast, does the wine run down the chins of all four? Why does "Mrs. Hathaway" look at her husband "as if for instructions" before she greets Captain Wilder?

TAG NAME?

There are endless jokes about the possibility that Anne Hathaway did have just that with William Shakespeare: When they married, she was twenty-six and pregnant; he was eighteen. Has Bradbury used Hathaway as a tag name for a character who, in both "—And the Moon Be Still as Bright" and "The Long Years," certainly hath a way too?

CHARACTERIZATION: HATHAWAY

Certainly he has had a way with science and technology that, in "Moon," solved the mystery of the Martians' mass death and, in our present story, has at least equalled the genius of Pikes and Stendhal in creating robots and a large-scale artificial environment. Technically, he might well be considered insane by some psychiatrists; they might view him as a split personality, able to act out—and need—an unreal situation that he can never forget is unreal. One counter argument is that preserving his wife and children in such a concrete detail has been an insane way of avoiding insanity. Programming his family" to be incapable of sadness shows he was well aware of his own limits; a robot crying might have pushed him over the edge into the abyss of total madness. It's also important to note that his robots serve a practical purpose, giving him more than his own two hands for chores like cooking, baking, and placing chairs around the table for Wilder's crew. He certainly is completely in touch with reality when Wilder's ship arrives. The way Wilder and Hathaway talk—disparagingly about Parkhill, knowingly about Wilder's having been kicked upstairs so he couldn't interfere with United States colonial policy on Mars—makes it clear that Wilder remembers Hathaway as something of a nonconformist.

CHARACTERIZATION: WILDER

He is still the near-perfect democratic leader, in control with just a nod or a word, willing to listen to alternatives, with none of the bitterness that welled up in him at the end of "—And the Moon Be Still as Bright," and at least no spoken bitterness now about his twenty-year exile. His final tribute to Hathaway speaks out in his being so touched by the robots' personalities that he can't destroy them and must even say a private good-bye to them.

THE TITLE

Hence, the title assumes a second meaning. For most of the story, it has referred to "the long years" of Hathaway's waiting. Now it refers also to the even longer years that the robots will go on functioning.

BRADBURY'S SOCIOPOLITICAL CRITICISM

Important clues to the author's own views: He notes that American-made buildings begin disintegrating in twenty years while the Martian structures have survived for millennia. America, presumably because it engaged in a nuclear war, has been destroyed while strange tongues that Hathaway cannot even identify now monopolize the radio waves. There has been no advance, in the midst of all this technological development, in management techniques: "They" are still kicking good people upstairs. Note, too, that by exiling a truly open mind like Wilder, they have left him in control after they have expired in their own mess.

SF

Bradbury has included in his futuristic world the double possibility of 1) strange viruses on other planets that could be fatal to Earth people, and 2) the evolution of familiar Earth viruses into new species on another planet. The one that kills off four of the five Hathaways is unknown to Doctor Hathaway himself. Is this the reverse of what happened to the Martians, who were killed off by the to-them-unknown chickenpox virus, carried by American explorers but not fatal to Americans? Has some slow-incubating Martian virus, unknown to Americans, infected them fatally? Or has the chickenpox virus evolved, during the rampage on Mars, into a stronger strain that now is fatal to humans?

BIBLE ALLUSION

When Hathaway says "Lazarus come forth," it has two or three levels of meaning in the current context. This was the phrase that Jesus used to summon his dead friend from his tomb (Gospel according to John, 11:43–44). Here it refers overtly to the chicken, frozen for twenty years, that Hathaway now calls into service, and covertly to the four members of his own family whom he called forth from the dead to be his sole companions. Does it refer, too, to the approaching rocket people, coming forth after a twenty-year absence from Mars?

THEMES

As usual, Bradbury is concerned with *mutation* and *metamorphosis*. Here, he especially explores the effects of solitude on human beings. Some, like Gripp, regard permanent solitude as desirable after a traumatic experience in romance. Most, like Hathaway, go to the limits of their ingenuity to fulfill their need for the company of their own kind.

COMPANION PIECES

Just as "The Long Years" is a companion piece for "The Silent Towns" in the sense that they both deal with people left behind on Mars, so "The Long Years" is a companion piece for the next story: they both deal with machines that, in ghostly fashion, ironically go on functioning after humanity has left them behind.

AUGUST 2026: THERE WILL COME SOFT RAINS

IMPORTANCE

This story is another Bradbury *tour de force*. It becomes a story, a complete story, even though it has only a setting. There is no human action. There are no characters. Yet, there is powerful characterization. In addition to that technical feat, this story has another claim to distinction. After Hiroshima and

Nagasaki, writers produced a plethora of stories predicting nuclear annihilation. Out of those hundreds, "There Will Come Soft Rains" is one of the few to survive as lasting literature.

LINKAGE
This story develops a motif that figured at the end of "The Long Years," when Hathaway's robots continue to function after all real human life is gone.

TITLE AND RELEVANCE
Bradbury names his story after the poem it quotes, which is titled "There Will Come Soft Rains," by Sara Teasdale. This poem appeared in her book *Flame and Shadow* (1920). Both the poem and book titles have relevance for Bradbury's story. The poem is based on a familiar theme of the Naturalist movement in literature (*Zolaism*): Nature is indifferent to humanity. Teasdale's version of the theme tells us spring will come again, with its soft rains, its sounds of birds and frogs, even if humanity has destroyed itself in a war. The poem is readymade for Bradbury's purposes. His allusion functions on three levels.

1. It underscores the situation in the story, in which nuclear war has removed the population from the scene.

2. It shows that as early as 1920, literature foresaw that possibility. As Marshall McLuhan put it, the writer is *the radar of humanity*, or the *antennae*, as Ezra Pound put it. Bradbury is reminding us that his story may also be prophetic.

3. Alluding to the poem also provides irony. In this 1920 version of annihilation via war, there are still birds and frogs left alive! But in 1950, just five years after Hiroshima, when Chronicles appeared, science already knew that maybe the only species to survive large-scale nuclear war would be the family Blattidae—the cockroaches.

SETTING

Although Bradbury doesn't name the exact area in which the story is set, we can infer it is a city surrounded by rural scenery, because foxes (as well as domestic animals) prowl the ruins, looking for a place to die. For purposes of plot and theme, Bradbury leaves just one house still standing, with its complex automation system still working.

SF

Bradbury's 2026 automated house is developed far beyond what we know, with our automatic garage doors, smoke detectors, and garbage disposals. In the Bradbury house, everything is automated, and all the automatic devices are centrally controlled and coordinated, it seems, by one mechanical brain. A voice on the stereo, e.g., not only announces the time, it also reminds the family what they should be doing at that moment. It even sets in motion the equipment they will need for their next activity.

BLACK HUMOR

Once again, Bradbury resorts to black humor so we can endure the basically tragic nature of the action. Much as the ruins make us want to cry, we can't help laughing over such phenomena as a cigarstand that is programmed to proffer, at a predetermined moment, a lighted cigar, presumably for the man of the house right after dinner.

CHARACTERIZATION

The former occupants (now atomized) are thus characterized by their house. They were "civilized" people whose technology was so far developed that it seems to have relieved them of even the slightest exercise of their muscles. We can imagine that the price they had to pay was enormous. They had to pace and synchronize their activities to the exact schedules set by the machinery. Leaving for work in the car, puffing that postprandial cigar, listening to Teasdale's poetry had all to be done at the exact time they were programmed for. Thus, humanity denied itself all chance of spontaneity and variation in its daily rounds. Even though the occupants owned Picasso canvases, it's clear the main characteristic of their lives must have been monotony, repetition; that is, death of the imagination.

METAPHOR AND SIMILE

Bradbury's talent for vivid imagery enjoys a ghoulish field day. As he expresses it, in this automated environment hundreds of mechanical attendants have been performing a religious ritual to honor the occupants who had become "gods." Indeed, even major appliances have become demigods: the incinerator *sits like evil Baal* (a major fertility god of ancient Semites, regarded as a satan by Hebrews and Christians). The heat of the fire *snaps mirrors like brittle winter ice.* Ironically, now that humans no longer exist, the fire takes on some human characteristics: it becomes clever in its fight with the fire-control system, and it even fingers the clothes in the closets. Bradbury's most powerful image is the one he uses to describe the effects that radiation has had on the outside wall of the house. The radiation charred the wall black except where it was blocked by human bodies, so that the family's silhouettes seem printed in white on a black surface—as in the negative of a photograph.

THEMES: THE ULTIMATE METAMORPHOSIS

Whitman predicted it. Seeing the proliferation of appliances in his day (1819–1892), he called his fellow Americans "amputees"—people who had voluntarily given up the use of their limbs so that machines could take their place. As anthropologists put it, man becomes what he admires and sees most of: here he himself has become a machine. Bradbury has developed this theme to the limit. Simply because humanity seemed compelled to build whatever it could build, it also used it, no matter how destructive "it" might have been.

POINT OF VIEW

In this chronicle Bradbury's plot has pre-determined his point of view. Here he cannot use his favorite camera angle, that of the author as limited narrator, because here there are no characters to whose perspective he can limit himself. So he chronicles that atomic aftermath from the point of view of the author omniscient.

PART 7

OCTOBER 2026: THE MILLION-YEAR PICNIC

BACKGROUND

This story appeared originally in the summer 1946 issue of *Planet Stories*. Although Bradbury placed it as the last story when he assembled the *Chronicles* (1950), it was actually the first piece to be written of all twenty-six works included here. It's as though Bradbury always had in mind that this was the piece that all the others had to aim toward. Indeed, it does pull together all the trends and themes of the previous twenty-five chronicles.

STRUCTURAL FUNCTION

The main action of the book, as we've explained earlier, ends with "There Will Come Soft Rains." At that point, Earth people, by the direct and indirect effects of their aggressive ways, have converted both Earth and Mars into "tomb planets." But to this mythic structure (described in Chapter 4, "Plot: Mythic Structure, Plus") Bradbury adds an epilogue (like a *coda*, a tailpiece, in music). Out of this vast cosmic devastation there emerges, safe and sane, just one family. Can they profit from the mistakes of the human race and, in this new environment on Mars, create the new kind of personality that will survive because it stresses human values?

TITLE

The title reminds us of Mrs. Parkhill spitefully telling her husband (in "The Off Season") that another "batch" of customers could be expected in a million years. In this present story, when the boy Robert asks "how far" they are going, Dad translates space into time and says "a million years." Then Bradbury himself calls the family outing "The Million-Year Picnic."

In "The Off Season," then, this huge time unit seems to stand for the period of time needed for humanity to recover, to get back to that point in evolution where it would again be capable of interplanetary travel: maybe never. And in this final story, "a million years" is Dad's way of saying either or both of two things: "We're going back a million years into Martian history," and, "Since we're blowing up our rocket, there's no thought of return, we're here Forever."

BRADBURY'S INGENIOUS CONCEPTION

Bradbury's genius in conceiving this story is in his vision that a great cosmic event like the death of Earth had best be viewed from the position of the smallest social unit—an isolated family, possibly the last of their species. He develops these two extremes in parallel: as the parents get on the radio the last sign of life on the home planet, they face the problem of how to tell the truth to the children. The final stroke of genius in story conception consists in Bradbury's decision to see the family drama from the point of view of the middle member of the five: the oldest boy, torn between trying to figure out what his parents are up to and trying to cushion the shock for his younger brothers. The action, then, really unfolds in contrapuntal fashion on five levels: development of the background situation on earth; discovery of the details about their new home planet; the parents' predicament; the oldest boy Timothy's trial: the younger boys' troubles in assimilating the truth.

FISH SYMBOLISM

The family all but forget the original excuse for the trip—that they were going fishing—but symbolically, that is just what they do do. The parents are fishing for the right words and moment to reveal the truth, they are all fishing in their own psyches for the appropriate reaction to their plight, they are all hunting for the city they like best. Notice that the one fish they do see also has symbolic meaning. The ring-fish has the power to surround its prey and assimilate it. In Dad's state of mind, he sees this creature as symbolic of the war that has engulfed and eaten humanity. And note too how Timothy sees his mother's thoughts swimming around in her eyes, like fish.

In most religions, and in-depth psychology, fish are fertility symbols, symbols of hope and vitality, partly because of their phallic shape, partly because of their lively activity in that primal element of all life, the water.

FIRE SYMBOLISM

Fire is an obvious but always powerful symbol of change and violence. One of Dad's important messages to the children is delivered via the papers he deliberately saves for their first Martian campfire. These papers symbolize aspects of human life on Earth that Dad hopes will never reappear on Mars: manipulation of the economy through purchase and sale of stocks and bonds; religious prejudice; antagonisms caused by the existence of national boundaries; war.

CHARACTERIZATION: THE EVIL MEN

Notice that a major portion of this story's suspense consists in Dad's uncertainty whether "the evil men" have really been left behind. These are the people who developed science too quickly, used it mainly for greedy wars and greedy colonization, the people Spender warned against, the people who exiled Wilder and set policy on Mars. Will they pursue the fugitive family? Do they still exist? It's part of the terror in this story that we have never seen any of the top evil men, only their grubby little pawns, like Parkhill. The psychological effect is comparable to that of *The Grapes of Wrath*, John Steinbeck's 1939 novel, in which the dispossessed farmers can never face their faceless antagonist: the Bank.

CHARACTERIZATION: TIMOTHY

Throughout the story Bradbury portrays with great sensitivity that stage in adolescence when a child begins to probe the mystique of family politics: the meaning of glances exchanged between adults, cautions expressed in just a word ("William!"), the meaning of an adult's tone of voice, the awful sense that adults know infinitely more than they reveal. The opening paragraph makes it clear that Timothy senses that Mom and Dad are putting a big scheme into motion. Unlike his brothers, Timothy is old enough to know that when Mom proposes a

fishing trip, she's really taking her cues from Dad. Timothy
fulfills the implicit trust his father has in him. He helps the
younger boys to understand the need for blowing up the
rocket and the great consolation Dad is conferring on them in
giving them an entire Martian city. Timothy's reward—note this
subtle development near the end—is that Dad tells him more
than he tells the others about his years of planning how to
escape Earth. In other words, Tim is now accepted into a man-
to-man relationship with his father. Timothy's conduct on this
day has initiated him into manhood adulthood.

CHARACTERIZATION: DAD

Bradbury makes him an ex-Governor (of Minnesota?) so that
his judgments in social and political matters carry greater
weight. Apparently, the vast numbers of his human relation-
ships on Earth left him little time to consider his family; one
of the differences that Timothy picks up is Dad's ability now
to give more of his attention to the boys. He is sensitive
enough to their needs now to ask them to pick the site on
Mars that they want for their new home. He is deliberate too
in enacting a series of nonverbal rituals—blowing up the family
rocket, burning the map of the world—that signify that they
cannot go back. His final ritual act is to carry out his mysterious
promise made earlier—to show them some Martians! No
words . . . just the sight of their own reflection in the canal—
gets the message across. Dad is wise enough to know that
important ideas must be ritualized as well as verbalized.

CHARACTERIZATION: MOM

One of Bradbury's most beautiful passages in this novel is the
one in which he describes how Mom looks back into Dad's
eyes to see what's ahead. The two parents have an intuitional
relationship: they are quietly tuned in to each other. Our main
criticism today, though, would be that she is too quiet. All the
major actions and statements are undertaken by Dad; at best
it seems they have agreed upon them in advance, but it's Dad's
show. If Bradbury were writing this story today (instead of
in 1946), he would without question give Mom a role more
commensurate with our concept of the equality of the sexes.

SF

One of the things the boys aren't old enough to understand is that in helping Mom they help their sister—still in the womb. In 1950, when Bradbury was completing this novel, it was not yet possible to determine the sex of a fetus so definitely. So here Bradbury racks up another SF prediction come true. And the silver ring-fish is totally his invention—a Mars fish apparently modeled on an amoeba, that is, a creature able to surround its food and thus assimilate it.

SETTING

The Martian landscape is still the standard Lowellian scene: a vast desert intersected by canals with the "dead cities" every few miles along the waterway. And once again Bradbury makes his point about hasty American construction: the cities abandoned by Americans in 2005 are already rotting into sawdust, while the ancient Martian buildings still stand in all their beauty.

TONE

This is probably Bradbury's most famous story, but it's not his best in the artistic sense of the word. Like "—And the Moon Be Still as Bright," it is a story of ideas. But "Picnic" appeals to us mainly as a set of ideas, whereas "Moon" appeals to us as a full experience, as much emotional as cerebral.

THEMES

The main message of "Picnic"—expressed in one of Bradbury's best-known sentences—comes in Governor Dad's saying that Earth's way of life *proved itself wrong and strangled itself with its own hands.* That is, it developed its knowledge faster in natural science than in the human sciences, and so humanity came to know everything about machines except how and why to use them wisely. Humanity's one hope lies in starting over on another planet, with all deliberate care to avoid the errors made back on Earth. And so Bradbury's master theme of metamorphosis is all-pervasive here, on several levels: Earth has died, Martian civilization has been wiped out by interplanetary contagion, Dad is more attentive to his family now, Timothy is trembling on the verge of full manhood, Mom is about to bear the first child born on Mars since the evacuation, and the stage is set for humanity's "second chance."

FINAL SUSPENSE: CHANCE

And indeed chance—both as opportunity and as Darwinian luck—is a big question mark at the end. Starting a new race on Mars depends largely on how lucky Dad's friends, the Edwards family, will be: Will their rocket make it safely too, with girls already thought of as "future wives" for Timothy, Michael, and Robert?

SELECTED BIBLIOGRAPHY

Aldiss, Brian W. Billion Year Spree: The True History of Science Fiction. Garden City, N.Y.: Doubleday, 1973; New York: Shocken, 1974.

Asimov, Isaac. *Asimov's Biographical Encyclopedia of Science and Technology.* Second revised edition. Garden City, NY: Doubleday, 1982.

Bretnor, Reginald, ed. *The Craft of Science Fiction.* New York: Harper & Row, 1976.

Bretnor, Reginald, ed. *Science Fiction, Today and Tomorrow.* New York: Harper & Row, 1974.

Clareson, Thomas D. *Voices for the Future.* Bowling Green University Popular Press, 1976.

Conger, Syndy McMillen. "Gothic Romance." *The Penguin Encyclopedia of Horror.* (*See* Sullivan, Jack.)

Elliot, Jeff. "The Bradbury Chronicles." *Future*, October 1978.

Feinberg, Gerald, and Robert Shapiro. *Life Beyond Earth.* New York: William Morrow, 1980.

Godwin, Francis. *The Man in the Moone: or a Discourse of a Voyage Thither By Domingo Gonsales the speedy Messenger.* London: 1638. (Reprinted in Smith College Studies in Modern Languages XIX, 1937.)

Greenberg, Martin H., and Joseph D. Olander, eds. *Ray Bradbury.* New York: Taplinger, 1980.

Gunn, James, ed. *The Road to Science Fiction.* Four volumes. New York: New American Library, 1979–1982.

————. *Alternate Worlds: The Illustrated History of Science Fiction*. Englewood Cliffs, N.J.: Prentice-Hall, 1975.

Hoskinson, Kevin. "*The Martian Chronicles* and *Fahrenheit 451*." *Extrapolation*, Winter 1995.

Hoyt, William Graves. *Lowell and Mars*. Tucson: University of Arizona Press, 1976.

Indick, Ben P. *The Drama of Ray Bradbury*. Santa Barbara: T-K Graphics, 1977.

Isherwood, Christopher. "Christopher Isherwood Reviews *The Martian Chronicles*." *Tomorrow*, October 1950.

Jacobs, Robert. "Interview with Ray Bradbury." *The Writer's Digest*, February 1976.

Johnson, Wayne L. *Ray Bradbury*. New York: Frederick Ungar, 1980.

————. "The Invasion Stories of Ray Bradbury." *Critical Encounters: Writers and Themes in Science Fiction*. (See Riley, Dick.)

Kelley, Ken. "The Playboy Interview." *Playboy*, May 1996.

Ketterer, David. *New Worlds for Old: The Apocalyptic Imagination*. Bloomington: Indiana University Press, 1974.

Lewis, Barbara. "Ray Bradbury, The Martian Chronicler." *Starlog*, August 1979.

Ley, Willy. *Watchers of the Skies*. New York: Viking, 1963.

Lowell, Percival. *Mars and its Canals*. New York: Macmillan, 1906.

————. *Mars as the Abode of Life*. New York: Macmillan, 1909.

Madsen, Axel. *John Huston.* Garden City, NY: Doubleday, 1978.

Miller, Walter James, ed. and trans. *The Annotated Jules Verne: From the Earth to the Moon.* New York: Crowell, 1978.

———, ed. *The Annotated Jules Verne:* Twenty Thousand Leagues under the Sea. New York: Crowell, 1976.

Moberg, David. "The Robotics Industry." *In These Times*, May 13, 1987.

Mogen, David. *Ray Bradbury.* Boston: Twayne, 1986.

Montaigne, Michel. *Essays.* Paris: 1580–1595. Available in numerous editions.

Moskowitz, Sam. *Seekers of Tomorrow, Masters of Modern Science Fiction.* New York: Ballantine, 1967.

Nolan, William F. *The Ray Bradbury Companion.* Detroit: Gale, 1975.

Peithman, Stephen, ed. *The Annotated Tales of Edgar Allan Poe.* Garden City, NY: Doubleday, 1981.

Rabkin, Eric S. "To Fairyland by Rocket: Bradbury's *The Martian Chronicles.*" *Ray Bradbury.* (See Greenberg, Martin.)

Rabkin, Eric S., ed. *Fantastic Worlds: Myths, Tales, Stories.* New York: Oxford, 1979.

Riley, Dick, ed. *Critical Encounters: Writers and Themes in Science Fiction.* New York: Frederick Ungar, 1978.

Rose, Mark, ed. *Science Fiction.* Englewood Cliffs, NJ: Spectrum, 1976.

Rottensteiner, Franz. The Science Fiction Book. New York: Seabury, 1975.

Scholes, Robert and Eric S. Rabkin. *Science Fiction: History, Science, Vision.* New York: Oxford, 1977.

Seed, David. The Flight from the Good Life. *Journal of American Studies,* August 1994.

Slusser, George Edgar. *The Ray Bradbury Chronicles.* San Bernardino, California: Borgo Press, 1977.

Sullivan, Anita T. "Ray Bradbury and Fantasy." *English Journal,* December 1972.

Sullivan, Jack, ed. *The Penguin Encyclopedia of Horror and the Supernatural.* New York: Viking Penguin, 1986.

Touponce, William F. "Some Aspects of Surrealism in the Work of Ray Bradbury." *Extrapolation,* Fall 1984.

Touponce, William F. *Ray Bradbury and the Poetics of Reverie: Fantasy, Science Fiction, and the Reader.* Ann Arbor, Michigan: UMI Research Press, 1984.

Valis, Noel. "*The Martian Chronicles* and Jorge Luis Borges." *Extrapolation,* Spring 1979.

Wilford, John Noble. "Mars Touted as Next U.S. Goal." *New York Times,* March 29, 1987. (Check *Times Index* for other articles on Mars.)

Wilson, Robert Scott, ed. *Those Who Can: A Science Fiction Reader.* New York: Mentor, 1973.

Wolhein, Donald A. *The Universe Makers.* New York: Harper & Row, 1971.

———, ed. *Men on the Moon.* New York: Ace, 1969.